Praise for *Let Faith Change Your Life*

We all have questions about faith, and Becky has answers. This book proves that God is relevant, relational, radical, and revolutionary when we keep the faith.

> Steve Arterburn
> Cofounder and Chairman
> Minirth Meier New Life Clinics

Becky makes faith real, practical, and authentic in our everyday living, regardless of our circumstances and starting points. All of us need to grow in faith.

> McKay Belk
> President, Merchandising
> Belk Stores Services, Inc.

Becky Tirabassi offers a personal, compelling look at faith in this very approachable book. For anyone who has wondered what was missing in life, or for those who are hesitant to take a closer look at God, *Let Faith Change Your Life* is a non-threatening view of a life-changing experience.

> Dale Hanson Bourke
> Publisher, Religion News Service

There is nothing more important in life than faith in God. Any tool that helps others get over their misconceptions and see faith as it is--relevant and relational--is a much needed resource in our country today. I'd encourage anyone to read *Let Faith Change Your Life*.

> J. Frank Harrison, III
> CEO, Coca Cola Consolidated, Inc.

Both men and women want to believe that faith will change their lives. Through the powerful true life stories and motivational principles presented in *Let Faith Change Your Life*, Becky Tirabassi proves that faith *does* change your life!

Coach Bill McCartney
Founder and CEO, Promise Keepers

For those who struggle to see God in their daily lives, Becky Tirabassi offers a refreshing new look at the power of simple faith.

Peggy Wehmeyer
ABC News Religion Correspondent

LET *F*AITH

CHANGE

YOUR

LIFE

**Other Books by Becky Tirabassi
from Thomas Nelson Publishers**

Let Prayer Change Your Life
Learn the unique approach to prayer that has revolutionized
communication with God for more than 100,000 people.

Let Prayer Change Your Life Workbook
Becky Tirabassi teaches you her exciting prayer system step-by-step
using self-tests, surveys, checklists, written prayer, and more.

My Partner Prayer Notebook
Develop a fresher, stronger, and more exciting relationship
with God using this unique prayer organizer, which has already sold
more than 150,000 copies.

Quietimes Student Prayer Journal
Help the teenagers in your life track their prayers and document
God's answers to build a solid, lifelong habit of talking with God.

LET AITH

CHANGE

YOUR

LIFE

BECKY TIRABASSI

THOMAS NELSON PUBLISHERS
Nashville • Atlanta • London • Vancouver

Published in Nashville, Tennessee, by Thomas Nelson, Inc., Publishers, and
distributed in Canada by Word Communications, Ltd., Richmond, British
Columbia.

Unless otherwise noted, Scripture quotations are taken from the HOLY
BIBLE, NEW INTERNATIONAL VERSION ®. Copyright © 1973,
1978, 1984 by International Bible Society. Used by permission of
Zondervan Publishing House. All rights reserved. Verses marked TLB are
taken from *The Living Bible*, copyright 1971 by Tyndale House Publishers,
Wheaton, IL. Used by permission. Scripture quotations noted KJV are from
the KING JAMES VERSION of the Bible.

Library of Congress Cataloging-in-Publication Data

Tirabassi, Becky, 1954–
    Let faith change your life / Becky Tirabassi.
      p.   cm.
    Includes bibliographical references.
    ISBN 0-7852-7235-6 (hardcover)
    1. Faith. 2. Tirabassi, Becky, 1954–. I. Title.
BT771.2.T5   1997
234'.2—dc20   96-35397
                                        CIP

Printed in the United States of America.

1 2 3 4 5 6 BVG 02 01 00 99 98 97

To
Jacob Allen Hunter
1917–1996

CONTENTS

A $\mathcal{R}$EVOLUTIONARY FAITH . . .

PREFACE

A FACT OF life is that no matter who we are, how old we are, where we live, who our parents are, or how much money we have, we will all experience some level of personal defeat, unmet expectation, disappointment, or the death of a friend or loved one. Sooner or later, we will reluctantly admit that life consists of many experiences, relationships, and circumstances that touch, even wound, our lives and our spirits. We "try everything" to ease the pain, to resolve issues, to change our lives! We struggle to help ourselves by turning to self-help books or organizations. Some of us attempt rigid religious rituals, or we go the other way and completely give up on developing and defining our spirituality . . . yet, deep inside, we know there is something missing.

I believe there comes a point or time in each of our lives when we search for something significant that offers hope and help and gives us the power to change ourselves, our circumstances, and our destiny! Our personal search differs from the next person's—the reason behind it, the depth to it, the amount of time we spend on it.

I have personally found and experienced only one solution that changed my life, and I am equally convinced that it *will change your life*! It is faith!

MY PERSONAL HOPE FOR YOU . . .

I have only one request as you read this book: try to ponder the faith I speak of without any preconceived ideas, expectations, or skepticism. My request is based on the conviction that any previous thoughts or experiences you have had that are attached to the word *faith* might . . .

1. be based on misconception.
2. have been wrought out of disappointment with God.
3. be caught behind intellectual barriers.
4. have been adversely affected by the impressions of certain people who have professed to be religious.
5. be disillusioned with mediocre or mundane spiritual experiences and exercises that left you empty.

I believe that any one of the above reasons could hinder you from embracing the faith that I am presenting! Therefore, I would like to encourage you to take a moment now to evaluate your past experiences with spirituality, religion, or the religious. Consider the good *and bad* religious experiences of your past. Do you have childhood memories of attending church? Did you partake in denominational exercises such as catechisms, baptism, or membership? Do you recall any "religious fanatics" who might have stepped into or over your boundaries? Or has the "church" as you know and define it only disappointed you?

Once you make a mental list of these memories, resolve to set them aside until the conclusion of this book. This simple step will harm no one, imply nothing, and yet allow you to have a clear and open mind to consider faith as relevant, relational, radical, and revolutionary.

If you and I were to meet in person and have a conversation, I am confident that you would not think of me as a stiff, stuffy, religious person. Instead, you would discover that my expertise has come from being a person who has lived the first half of life *without* real faith and the second half (a total of forty-two years) *with* a faith that has indeed changed my life.

I am aware that there are already a multitude of self-help books, New Age concepts, and scientific theories out there telling you how to make necessary changes, feel loved, or become successful. But I have written *Let Faith Change Your Life* for one reason: I am hopeful that if you see the faith that I speak of through the eyes of someone other than a theologian, parent, clinician, professor, or New Age teacher, you will seriously consider faith and *let it change your life!*

LET *F*AITH

CHANGE

YOUR
LIFE

A RELEVANT FAITH . . .

MEETS YOU RIGHT WHERE YOU ARE AT!

BEFORE THE EVENING lecture ever began, I got separated from my husband, Roger, but I had not lost sight of Rick, my only and older brother. We never did locate Roger, so we just sat together in the rear left section of the room.

The guest speaker was a small, tan, middle-aged, white-haired man with a collegiate "air." He was very casually dressed in loafers, khakis, button-down shirt, and crewneck sweater. His baritone voice was enthralling, and his humorous style of communicating was very enjoyable. His most captivating strength, though, was his mesmerizing personal story.

He had been a priest for most of his life, but his struggle with alcohol had literally lowered him to the demeaning depths of a "gutter" alcoholic. As his story unfolded, it developed into a powerful message of healing, hope, and restoration.

By the end of the lecture, each listener sat riveted to his or her seat, appearing spellbound, obviously deeply touched, just as I had been. Perhaps we were unwilling to lose the emotion of the moment by getting up or leaving the room. Maybe we just didn't want the healing power of this story to lose its impact upon our lives or be quickly forgotten with the hurry and hustle of an unruly parking lot.

It was unspoken, but we all seemed to understand: if a priest could fall so low and find such a hope-filled way out, so could I . . . so could you . . . so could anyone.

The room was whisper quiet. Then slowly, a few people journeyed to the front of the room to embrace the speaker. Soon, others stood in little groups, anxious to paraphrase and personalize the message they had just heard.

Eventually, Rick and I stood up to look for my husband. Reluctantly, I began the arduous task of looking at every head. (My search procedure has become easier through the years, since my husband is now bald!)

As my eyes traveled from the left side to the middle section of the room, I spotted a fellow, about my age, sitting by himself. For some reason he caught my attention, probably because the room was so full of mingling and mixing. A lone "sitter" just seemed out of place. I mentioned this to my quiet, shy brother.

"Rick," I said, "I wonder why that guy is sitting alone? Maybe he needs to talk?"

"I'm sure he's just waiting for someone," my brother replied.

"I doubt that. You don't wait sitting down. You wait standing up," I murmured, while a flurry of thoughts and reasons for his "loneliness" flashed through my type A mind.

I can't explain why this man initially caught my attention or why I couldn't seem to shake the thought that he might want to talk to someone, but again I mentioned it to my brother, "Maybe we should just go over and talk to him?"

"What would you say?" Rick asked nervously. I could hear a familiar uneasiness in his voice that signaled he was uncertain of what I might be getting us into.

"Well . . ." I hesitated. Then it hit me! If this guy was anything like my brother, I should ask *my brother* what words might start up a conversation with a shy guy! Rick had been living with us for about six months. Like so many of us who were born in the 1940s and 1950s, he was struggling to make sense of his past and understand his role in the Vietnam War. He was currently in the process of making a "midlife" occupational change.

Believing that California offered him opportunities for spiritual, mental, and emotional growth, my husband and I had invited Rick to come live with us. He had finally accepted our invitation. By this point, he was anxiously looking for a job and a place of his own in which to live. So I asked Rick, "What do *you* think I should say?"

He thought a moment and replied, "You could ask him if he's okay."

"Good idea!" I agreed. Now that my brother was comfortable with what I was going to ask the man, I knew it would be easy to get Rick to walk over there with me! So I nonchalantly offered a bit of strategy: "Let's walk over to the middle section, then down the row in front of him. When we get *right* in front of him, let's turn toward him and I'll ask him if he's *okay!*"

With a nod of agreement, Rick walked with me to the middle section of the meeting room. (By this time, I had forgotten that I was even looking for my husband!) When we were directly in front of the man, I quickly assessed by his hair color, glasses, and casual dress that he was in his forties, just as Rick and I were. This boosted my confidence that we could start a friendly conversation. Observing more closely, though, I noticed that his demeanor was very sad, and though I couldn't tell if he had been crying, it was obvious that he was emotional. I simply started our conversation with the question, "Are you okay?"

He took a minute before he replied, then answered slowly, "I haven't been to church in twenty years." My heart just about stopped beating. He continued, "This past year, I lost my job, my wife left me, I lost my home . . . , and having never been much of a drinker before, I became such an alcoholic that I've been in a treatment center for the past few months."

"What's your name?" I asked.

"Peter," he replied.

I immediately gave my brother the look that inferred, "Shall we have a seat?"

Slowly lowering ourselves into seats in front of Peter, we turned toward him and made eye contact. I responded to his obviously difficult introduction of himself with, "Well, you've just heard the most amazing story by one of the greatest speakers I've ever heard, and isn't it incredible how it relates to your circumstances?"

Even as I said those words, I marveled at the fact that I, a former alcoholic, was the *one person out of the fifteen hundred people* in that room who was compelled to talk with this perfect stranger! How much more relevant could the circumstances become? I wondered. It was beginning to feel like part of a predestined plan.

Initially, Peter seemed embarrassed to say much more, then after a few moments he went on with his story: "For the past few weeks I've watched people come into this building. You see, I'm ashamed to say this, but since I've lost everything, I've been living across the street . . . with my sister."

Shrugging my shoulders and pointing to my brother, I kidded, "Don't feel so bad. He lives with his sister!" We all smiled.

Then his eyes shifted away from our faces and down into his lap. He paused, then continued quietly, "I wouldn't want anyone *here* to know that I am an alcoholic."

My eyes filled with tears. As sincerely as I could, I said to him, "Peter, I'm an alcoholic, too!"

His startled look spoke more than words, intimating that I might be lying, because I didn't have the appearance or actions of an alcoholic.

I felt it was time to briefly share my own story . . .

"In 1976, I hit bottom after six years of drugs and alcohol and immorality. In August of that year, I began to seriously consider suicide. But in a desperate last effort to find relief from my despair, I drove to a church. I didn't know the name of the church or the pastor, but the janitor of the church found me and talked with me! *After* I told him what a mess my life was, he said, 'God loves you just the way you are.'

"At first, I was taken by surprise. It seemed impossible that anyone could love me, much less God. (My perception of God at that time was very authoritarian and punishing.) But I wanted—and needed—to believe that someone could still love me. So, I listened to every word that this stranger shared about God. Even when he quoted Scripture, I wasn't offended because the words were so very hope-filled and comforting.

■ ■ ■

It seemed impossible that anyone could love me, much less God.

■ ■ ■

"As Ralph, the janitor, explained how much God wanted to have a relationship with me, I could admit that my drugs and alcohol and their consequences had separated me from God—and just about everyone else. Soon, I was confessing to Ralph just how despicable my life had gotten. I had even considered getting professional help and made repeated, weak attempts to help myself, but nothing worked. That was when the janitor boldly told me that God was the *only One* who could help me out of my deep despair, addiction, and humiliation. I certainly couldn't deny that I *needed* help. And I had absolutely nowhere else to turn.

"Peter," I continued, sharing words from my past while using my eyes to show him how deeply I identified with him, "in 1976, the janitor who shared with me spoke very similar words to those the speaker used tonight. He told me that reconciliation with God is the only way to experience true freedom from guilt and shame. He encouraged me to let God be the person to give me the power to overcome my addictions. He asked me if I would like to confess with my mouth and believe with my heart that Jesus lived in history, died on a cross, and rose from the dead to reconcile me—a sinner—to God the Father because He loved me!

"On August 26, 1976, I said a simple prayer, much like the prayer you heard the former priest offer tonight . . . 'Dear Lord, come into my heart. I can't go on living like this. I need Your help to change. Forgive me for the way I've been living and running and hurting myself, others, and You. I believe that You love me, Jesus, and that You died on the cross to save me. I want to love You and be loved by You. Please come into my life and give me a fresh start. Make me new. Fill me up with Your Holy Spirit.'

"I said those words almost twenty years ago and—as my brother is a witness to what I've just told you—that day was the beginning of a whole new life! The story you heard the former priest tell tonight and my story—and *your* story—are the *same* stories. We *all* have been separated from God. Everyone is or has been, in different ways and at various times.

"Peter, you don't need to be afraid or ashamed to tell people that you are hurting or that you need help. In fact, this place has a Twelve-Step meeting on Wednesday nights that is similar to a typical recovery program where two hundred to three hundred people attend regularly!"

He couldn't believe that a church would have a public meeting for people who admitted they had problems! He looked at my brother and asked, "Have you ever been to the Twelve-Step program here?" Rick gave me the "I knew you'd get me into something" look, but proceeded to answer, "Yes, I have."

Peter asked, "Would you go with me sometime?" Rick nodded yes—hesitantly—but it was a yes!

By this point, it was obvious to all of us that our conversation was no coincidence and this meeting was not by chance. There was even more to come.

Peter said, "If I could only pray." It was apparent that he had been struggling with wanting to know and understand God, perhaps even solicit His help, but was unsure of where or how to begin! How could I tell him without totally freaking him out that for the previous five years, my full-time traveling occupation had been to *teach and motivate people to pray*? I just said, "Well, you've come to the right place."

Before the week was over, Peter had learned how to pray! We loaded him up with books and tapes and *more* than enough support and understanding to encourage him in his recovery process. And he now had a regular place to grow spiritually—right across the street from his sister's house!

When I last saw Peter, he enthusiastically told me that he was very involved in spiritual growth groups, had acquired a good job, and had made several new friends! In fact, he was excited that his sister and her fiancé had seen such a difference in *his* life that they, too, had begun their own search for God!

He added that he was extremely grateful that a stranger had been bold enough to reach out and share Christ with him at such a low point in his life! I told him that I could relate to that feeling!

How could faith be so relevant to such a diverse group of individuals as a former priest, a stockbroker, and an alcoholic young woman? Because we had each experienced common fears. We were afraid that . . .

no one could love us,

no one could trust us,

no one could respect us, and

no one could ever forgive us.

At points when we couldn't have been more imperfect or undeserving, faith *met us,* lifted us, offering us escape— and hope for change! Faith in a forgiving God was the answer for a broken priest who was supposed to teach faith, yet had failed. It rescued a yuppie stockbroker who lost all hope for living when his dreams and plans were shattered through an unexpected divorce and hard times. And the very *same* faith brought much-needed change to a hopeless, addicted twenty-one-year-old woman. Along with millions of others throughout all time, we experienced faith to meet us *right where we were at*—even before we were able to make changes or clean up our lives!

■   ■   ■

At points when we couldn't have been more imperfect or undeserving, faith *met us*, lifted us, offering us escape—and hope for change!

■   ■   ■

Though I've spoken of a priest, a stockbroker, and an alcoholic who were dramatically changed by faith, don't be misled to believe that faith is only relevant to the emotionally broken person.

Faith meets the successful person, who appears to "have it all" on the outside, yet on the inside admits there is a missing piece.

Faith meets the intellectual man and woman and provides solid answers to their questions.

Faith meets those who sincerely want to know their eternal fate.

Faith meets those with misconceptions.

A $\mathscr{R}$ELEVANT
FAITH . . .

MEETS THOSE WHO
ARE SUCCESSFUL

I N 1990, I ventured out on an entirely new dream! I decided to produce a step aerobics video, but choreographed to all Christian music. It was a product that I thought could really fill a need. Though I was inexperienced in the video-making business, I had been enthusiastically teaching aerobics in a large southern California health club for the previous four years.

After almost a year, all of the pieces had fallen together to produce *Step into Fitness,* except for hiring a choreographer. I felt that entering into a primarily secular industry with a Christian-related product was risky in itself, so I hoped to convince a nationally known aerobics choreographer to give this video the professional look and credibility it would need to meet the high standards of the fitness industry.

To find that special person, I called an international fitness organization, and a representative suggested that I contact "Fitness Instructor of the Year," Candice Copeland-Brooks, who lived in Los Angeles. Her credentials were a mile long! She had a series of her own fitness videos, she appeared in numerous magazine advertisements and articles, her international popularity was soaring, she was sponsored by Reebok—and she has since been on the cover of *Shape* magazine! What more could you ask for?

In order to meet her, I attended one of her workshops and introduced myself, immediately asking if she was interested in choreographing a "Christian music" fitness video. The fitness industry at that time had a strong "New Age" image, so I was a little nervous about inviting her to be a part of a project that was going to have Christian music with Christian cameramen, instructors, and producers involved in it. I kept mentioning that everything about the video would be "Christian." Finally, she asked me, "What do you think I am . . . an atheist?" I laughed uncomfortably and realized that time would tell!

Over the year that it took to choreograph and film the video, Candice began to explain her spiritual past and current "search for meaning." She grew up in a Catholic family and had spent many years in parochial school, catechism, and high school church youth groups. As long as she could remember, she had known all about God, Jesus, and the Holy

Spirit, attending two or three Masses on Sundays, well into college.

In her own words, she said, "What amazed me is that, with all this 'religion' in my life, I somehow never grasped the ideas (1) that God loves me more than I will ever comprehend, and (2) that a relationship with Christ is the way to salvation and eternal life.

"I moved into an apartment my second year in college and immediately stopped going to church. In spite of not going to church, I felt a strong spiritual desire within me . . . I just didn't know where to find what was missing. Looking back, I remember taking college electives such as World Religions and The Bible as Literature. I explored Eastern religions and listened to others talk about different religions. I still didn't find what I was looking for.

"I got married in my early twenties and left my husband after a year and a half because he was no longer interested in a monogamous marriage relationship. I immediately got into a series of equally destructive relationships and tried to excel at my work. I was traveling about fifteen days a month then, speaking at conventions for fitness professionals. No matter how well my workshops went, or how many compliments I got, I felt no satisfaction. I sat on an airplane one night and prayed, 'God, please help me out of this rat race and find me a relationship that works.'

"God listened, and I found the most important relationship in my life . . . Christ. But God first sent some other people into my life to help me find Him. First, I met the most wonderful man in the world . . . my husband, Douglas, who was also on a spiritual search. In the next few years I also met two women whom I know God put into my life to help me make changes.

"I met Patty in Washington, D.C., early one morning while out running before a fitness convention. We immediately clicked and our friendship progressed over the next few weeks. One day we were talking about spiritual backgrounds, and I asked her why she seemed different from me. She answered that I had religion, but not a relationship with Jesus. A few months after that I met Becky Tirabassi, who explained that she was a Christian author and motivational speaker, and wanted to tap into the Christian fitness market.

"Becky gave me a book she had written about the power of prayer. It explained how to ask the Lord into your life and what salvation meant. I went out and bought a Bible . . . my first, then got on my knees and confessed my sins and asked Jesus to come into my life. It was the most powerful thing that has ever happened to me. I knew immediately that this was what had been missing!"

Candice, now forty years old, was recently baptized. Whenever given the opportunity, she openly shares how Christ met her right where she was at. Looking back at her life before Christ and since, she said, "This was six years ago, and I still thank Him daily for being patient with me, and for putting people into my life who helped direct me to Him. God has given me a passion to want to share the gospel with others, even though it is scary sometimes to do that.

"I am continually amazed at how He works through me, and I feel so much clearer about my purpose in life. I don't need to please everyone else all of the time . . . because I know God loves me no matter what. I can joyfully serve others now because I am not doing it just for their approval. In my work as a public speaker and fitness instructor I no longer seek personal approval and applause. Instead I pray that Christ's light will shine through me and touch some of those people who thought they came to learn about fitness. I feel a peace and a freedom that I never had before because I know now that I don't have to be in control of everything in my life. I just need to look to Him to open the right doors, and all I have to do is walk diligently through them and give God the glory for making things turn out the way they should.

"To sum it all up, I know we all have a lot of choices. But because of Christ in my life, I choose submission to Him rather than trying to control my life. I choose joy in Him rather than worry, and I choose peace in Him rather than approval and applause from others."

I met Candice when she was very successful. Today she is still a very successful leader in the fitness industry, but no longer has a missing piece! She and her husband attend a great church and are a part of a spiritual growth group. Candice teaches Sunday school, her kids attend a combination of Christian and home schools, and she often blends her faith with fitness!

Faith was relevant to Candice six years ago when she was successful and searching—and it is still relevant to her today as a wife, a mother, and a professional!

3

A

ℛELEVANT

FAITH . . .

MEETS THOSE WHO
ARE INTELLECTUAL

I HAVE MET many people who simply discount faith because they do not consider it true and factual, cannot get past the "evolution versus creation" debate, or feel that faith is primarily for the emotionally inclined or needy.

In fact, in one of my more memorable encounters, I was sworn at by a lawyer on an airplane. After I had a twenty-minute conversation with him on the relevance of faith, he bellowed out loud, "You're full of ____, and I don't respect you." (Over the next two hours, he and I did become friends.)

But I have observed that the philosophical or analytical person struggles more with giving in to faith on an intellectual level than most other personalities. Therefore, when a famous person in politics or business has a faith encounter, it is worth telling the story to encourage those of similar mind, education, background, or reservation.

■   ■   ■

The philosophical or analytical person struggles more with giving in to faith on an intellectual level than most other personalities.

■   ■   ■

Most of us know something about the Watergate scandal in the 1970s and its fallout. Charles Colson was one of the men involved who—though extremely indomitable and intellectual—fell to the tyranny of power.

At the height of his career in politics and law, he said he had never considered Jesus Christ as more than "an historical figure, a prophet, a cut above His time." He could not fathom how an intelligent, successful businessman could accept God and commit his life to Him. In an exclusive interview published in the February 1976 *Moody Monthly* magazine, Chuck Colson said, "My biggest problem had always been the intellectual reservations. I knew there was a God, but I could never see how man could have a personal relationship with Him."

Colson had once considered faith in God to be "pure Pollyanna." Even as his world was crashing in around him, he could not just turn his life over to God. He found it incredulous that accepting Christ meant simply asking Him into your life. But a businessman whom Chuck respected, Tom Phillips, challenged him to read *Mere Christianity* by C. S.

Lewis. Chuck had watched how the faith experience had changed the man's life. Tom knew that Chuck had considered Jesus only a historical figure, but explained to him that a person couldn't have a relationship with someone he didn't believe was still alive.

In his book *Born Again,* Chuck tells of the night in Tom Phillips's home when Tom asked him if he was ready to accept Christ. Chuck admitted that at that invitation, he hesitated, saying, "I can't tell you I'm ready to make that kind of commitment. I've got to be certain. I've got intellectual hang-ups to get past. How can I make a commitment now? My whole world is crashing down around me. I've got to answer all the intellectual arguments first."

■ ■ ■

His heart had been deeply touched by a loving, forgiving God who met him and loved him just the way he was, right where he was at!

■ ■ ■

Chuck read C. S. Lewis's book, expecting it to reach a reader on an emotional level. Instead, he found "an intellect so disciplined, so lucid, so relentlessly logical that I could only be grateful that I had never faced him in a court of law."

After considering Christ's claims and realizing that he wouldn't question legal principles with less historical validity, Colson faced the proposition that Jesus is God. But could he accept Him? He convinced himself that he could—and his life changed forever.

Only afterward would he be indicted for his part in Watergate and sent to prison. No longer a politician, Colson, convinced of the relevance of faith in *any* person's life, began an organization called Prison Fellowship. The fellowship is now twenty years old. Though he was—and is—a brilliant scholar and lawyer who needed his intellectual questions satisfied, his heart had been deeply touched by a loving, forgiving God who met him and loved him just the way he was, right where he was at! What he realized about faith was that it was relevant to *all* men and women, whether they possessed great intellect and power—or very little.

4

A
ℛELEVANT
FAITH . . .

MEETS THOSE
FACING DEATH

So many of us wondered as little children if we were "good enough to get into heaven." The answer to that question always seemed elusive. By our teen years, most of us had done enough "bad things" that we grew more—rather than less—worried and uncertain about our eternal fate. For some of us, this led to further distance from spiritual things. Others of us still feverishly try to make up for our past mistakes by doing good, giving money, or ritualistically or periodically attending church services! But nothing ever seems to fully take away the insecurity looming over those of us who grasp for eternity through good deeds or clean consciences. Something deep within us keeps trying to "get to heaven," though we can't fathom all that we'd have to do to be right with a holy God!

In theory, both the insecure and the dying person ask the same question, "How can I know if I'm going to go to heaven?" They want answers to questions, such as, Where will I go when I die? What will "life after death" be like? Will I receive punishment or reward?

At no other time *than at the point of death* does faith become more relevant, whether for yourself, for someone you love, or for the family whose child is dying. We long to . . .

- make sense of death,
- have concrete answers for the unknown,
- receive hope and, ultimately,
- understand our destiny with certainty.

Unexpectedly, this past April, my father suffered a severe heart attack, went into a coma, and was near death. The thought of not being with him or ever talking to him again prompted all three Hunter kids to hop on the first planes out of California and into Cleveland by Monday to join our mom's bedside vigil.

My dad awoke on Tuesday morning, against all odds, and thankfully we were all there. By taking shifts of sitting next to him, holding his hand, sleeping in the lobby at night, and easing his concerns each time he woke up confused, we became united in a common goal to nurse him back to health and move him out to California to be closer to us. Even though he was seventy-nine years old, he repeatedly told us that he didn't really *want* to leave his five-day-a-week bookkeeping job at the Cleveland Youth for Christ (YFC) office, his familiar coffee-drinking buddies at Bob's Big Boy, his twenty-year-old church family, his dog, or his roots. He also mentioned that he wanted to be buried beside his parents' grave site in Cleveland.

But by Friday, my dad had improved so much, he was moved from CCU to a step-down unit. We were thrilled at his miraculous recovery.

I spent all day Friday with him. We chatted a lot about the past, his meticulous bookkeeping for the previous thirteen years, and how much he loved his kids, his wife, and the Cleveland Indians (who had won the American League Championship Title in 1995 after a forty-year drought!). Because the Cleveland Indians game was on television that night, he and I decided that we should make an "evening" out of watching the game. So, I briefly went home to shower and eat and hurried back to watch the game alone with Dad, while the rest of the family rested from the emotional drain of the week.

At 7:05 P.M., Dad and I turned on the television to watch our Indians play the Toronto BlueJays in the Skydome. We were especially thrilled that the starting pitcher was Orel Hershiser, a Christian athlete who had often shared his faith with kids at Youth for Christ sponsored events.

With each play, we added our colorful commentary— laughing, complaining, and second-guessing the good and bad plays and calls.

At game's end, I told my dad that I was going to sleep at

the house that night, rather than the hospital. Since he was coming home next week, I reminded him that I would be staying in Cleveland until Sunday, Rick would leave on Monday, and my older sister, Reggie, would stay until Tuesday. "All right," he said.

My dad had told me that he prayed every night, so I asked him if I could pray a special prayer for him. As sweet as I could ever imagine, my dad clasped his hands around mine, and I prayed out loud for God to be near him, watch over him, and take good care of him.

As I left the hospital room at 11:00 P.M., I heard my dad ask the nurse, "Did you hear that nice prayer my daughter prayed for me?"

Starting back in 1976 when I introduced my family to a personal relationship with Christ, the last twenty years of my dad's life had been much more full of God, family, sobriety, and his love for his work at YFC than his first fifty-nine years. Both he and his father had been alcoholics, but in 1971, he quit drinking after a stroke. Life *without* alcohol and *with* God was much happier and fulfilling for all of the Hunters! And we were all looking forward to more years together.

■ ■ ■

Life *without* alcohol and *with* God was much happier and fulfilling.

■ ■ ■

At 6:30 A.M. on Saturday, we received a call from the hospital that my father had had another heart attack. The four of us immediately got in the car and drove the short distance to the hospital. When we entered my dad's hospital room at 6:45 A.M., a nurse was waiting for us next to my father's still body.

She said, "Jacob had three heart attacks this morning. The trauma team tried many times to resuscitate him, but he never woke up. We feel confident that he never felt the heart attacks. He actually died in his sleep."

Since my childhood, my father told the family how he would die. He always said that he would just not wake up one morning. That was exactly what happened.

We, of course, were stunned by the timing of his death, but not surprised that he died. He had been struggling with emphysema and just couldn't seem to quit smoking.

Probably because my dad had been on fewer medicines, he was much more expressive, talkative, and alert than he had been for the previous year. His numerous comments about how proud he was of each of his children, his gentle touches and hand squeezes, as well as the hourly look and words of love and affection that were overwhelmingly missing in my childhood, in one week filled the huge hole in my heart and made up for all those lost years. I didn't want to let go of them so quickly. My heart, though, was compassionate enough to understand that my dad did not want to move or suffer any longer. I wasn't mad at God. I couldn't deny how we were all given one week of great memories with my dad. But having never planned a funeral or experienced the death of a close relative, I walked through the day either emotionally

25

numb or completely tearful. In my heart of hearts, I did not want to lose my dad yet. That previous week had been one of the most healing times of my life.

By late afternoon, the reality of my dad's death was sinking in. That was when it occurred to me to look at the *Cleveland Press* sports page. The bold headline read as follows:

LEAP OF FAITH
FEELS LIKE HOME.

The first line of the Cleveland Indians' article said, "Has the Skydome turned into Jacob's Field?" My father's name, his father's name, as well as my son's name, is Jacob. I was immediately in shock. I did not think this was a coincidence. I felt that this was truly meant for me to read and emotionally connect with!

I reasoned that of all nights for me and Dad to watch the Indians game, how interesting that they were playing in the SKYDOME! Because so many Cleveland fans could not buy seats in their home stadium, JACOB'S FIELD, they were driving up to the Toronto SKYDOME in mass numbers. Thus, the article began, "Has the Skydome turned into Jacob's Field?" It made me think that my dad, Jacob, and his dad, Jacob, were together in heaven—a skydome! Furthermore, I sensed that Dad had a little message for me: going to heaven was a LEAP OF FAITH and it FEELS LIKE HOME! I've saved that sports page. And I am confident that my dad is in his heavenly home—waiting for us!

Late on the day that my dad died, April 27, my husband called from California to ask if I had read my *One Year Bible* yet. I hadn't. (For many years, my husband and I have daily read the *One Year Bible*. It divides the entire Bible into 365 readings, enabling a person to read through the whole Bible in a year. Each day's assigned reading includes a portion of the New Testament, Old Testament, Psalms, and Proverbs.)

He said, "Go get your Bible, and read today's verses. You won't believe what it says!" The last verse of that day's New Testament reading was Luke 23:43: "And Jesus replied, 'Today you will be with me in Paradise. This is a solemn promise'" (TLB).

■ ■ ■

Faith gives us confidence to rejoice in the gift of eternal life rather than regret the bodily death at the end of temporal earthly life.

■ ■ ■

Again, I sensed that my heavenly Father wanted to assure me—on the very day that my dad left this earth—that he had gone right to his heavenly home to be with Jesus. I was also comforted in knowing that though I will miss him on earth, I will someday be reunited with him in heaven. With death, there are temporary sadness and pain to deal with, but those who have put their faith in Jesus have an eternal promise that they will be with Him in paradise. Faith gives us confidence to rejoice in the gift of eternal life rather than regret the bodily death at the end of temporal earthly life.

Death is inevitable for everyone, but those who possess faith in the God of the Bible need not fear death. We may face and understandably fear pain, but we do not have to fear the grave. At the moment we believe in Christ, the Bible says that we receive eternal life—as a gift, not earned or deserved, but paid for by Christ's substitutionary death on the cross. A relevant faith understands that life on earth is temporal, not eternal, but life after earth continues through eternity with God.

5

A
ℛELEVANT
FAITH . . .

MEETS THOSE WITH
MISCONCEPTIONS

C. S. LEWIS wrote in *Mere Christianity,*

I have been asked to tell you what Christians believe, and I am going to begin by telling you one thing that Christians do not need to believe. If you are a Christian you do not have to believe that all the other religions are simply wrong all through. If you are an atheist you do have to believe that the main point in all the religions of the whole world is simply one huge mistake. If you are a Christian, you are free to think that all these religions, even the queerest ones, contain at least some hint of the truth.

But, of course, being a Christian does mean thinking that where Christianity differs from other religions, Christianity is right and they are wrong. As in arithmetic—there is only one right answer to a sum, and all other answers are wrong: but some of the wrong answers are much nearer being right than others.

I've had many conversations with people who become irate when confronted with the concept that there is only one way to God. They shrivel and wretch at the thought of needing a Savior, calling themselves a sinner, or believing that a good God could create hell. They refuse to believe, and they reject biblical teaching. Instead, they often resort to a kinder, gentler concept of God and the universe. They mix and match beliefs. They discount some truths while keeping other, more palatable approaches to life and faith. This process creates constant barriers to a relevant faith because it perpetuates misconceptions about the God of the Bible.

As a teenager, one of the reasons I avoided the exploration of faith in my life was that I thought faith was only for the piously perfect or ridiculously dull. And though I knew I wasn't perfect, I refused to be dull!

■   ■   ■

Faith gave me the courage and confidence to hope
and dare to live a different life.

■   ■   ■

As a young adult, I pushed faith away because I feared that it would forcefully take over, "fix me up," or "straighten me out." Ironically, when I finally relinquished my fears and gave in to faith, it gave me the courage and confidence to hope and dare to live a different life from what I was living at the moment, not just in twenty years or if I sobered up or became good.

For many years I thought faith was reserved only for

religious services, religious holidays, or the clergy. I was most surprised to find that faith was practical for daily living, and that it provided promises, precepts, and a Person to guide me through each day, not only if I measured up, but even when I was struggling.

■ ■ ■

Faith provided promises, precepts, and a Person to guide me through each day.

■ ■ ■

I quickly learned that a relevant faith does not require us to live a constrained, unhappy, or legalistic life. Instead, faith allows us to lead a supernatural lifestyle *not guided by superstition, chance, or luck,* but guided by a living, loving, and present God.

In fact, people with a relevant faith will actively search, look for, invite, and expect God to intervene on their behalf and guide them, rather than rely on horoscopes, stock reports, or lucky charms to do the same.

A relevant faith lives within the framework that God is as real as our best friend or wisest counselor, *only* all-knowing, all-powerful, and always present. Once we believe that God is present in our lives, we can begin to live supernaturally in our environment, expecting that He will and can guide us by . . .

- giving us motivating thoughts, new ideas, and exciting dreams to pursue.
- instructing us through His written Word, the Bible.

31

- orchestrating events on our behalf.
- opening avenues of opportunity for us.
- directing us through another's timely advice.

When you are convinced that faith is more than an idea or "it," that it is being *loved* by Someone who can help, renew, empower, improve, forgive, and meet you in your darkest moments, it becomes the most relevant resource you have to change your life!

6

A
$\mathscr{R}$ELATIONAL
FAITH . . .

IS A GREAT DEBATE:
RELIGION
OR RELATIONSHIP?

IN THE 1960s, going to college had a commonality to it. Most everyone from the Youngstown area enrolled in one of Ohio's large state schools—Bowling Green, Kent State, or Ohio State—often, to major in education. All the guys dressed the same preppy way: button-down collars, V-neck sweaters, saddle shoes or penny loafers, and tailored sport jackets. They drove Chevrolets and joined fraternities with the expectation of fraternizing with the "sisters" of the sororities.

Ted was no different. In fact, all the pieces fell into place . . . right up to "the girl." He was a Sigma Chi; she was a Delta Gam. They had naturally gravitated to each other—

having been raised in the same religion, with the same ethnic background, and being from the same hometown. At the beginning of their senior year, they were lavaliered, and by spring, they were pinned. And being accepted into graduate school to get a master's in education and counseling gave Ted the perfect end to a picture-perfect college career! A June wedding was planned.

Upon graduating and marrying, Ted and Patty took jobs in Youngstown. They bought a home, settled in a middle-class community, and busily began to lead separate lives. They pursued their own careers, planning to wait a few years before having children. Excelling in their fields, they worked days and evenings, networking and climbing the "rungs" of their ladders. Unfortunately, neither of them considered this pattern a troubling sign in their relationship.

Over the next year, Patty was involved in her work as much as Ted was in his, but her time away from home seemed to add distance to their relationship when they were together. Ted wondered if the newness of marriage was wearing off or if he might be putting in too many extra hours at school by counseling *and* teaching. He wouldn't even let himself speculate that they might be growing apart or have very little left in common. But something was very wrong. When he finally asked her what was wrong, it was virtually too late. She had been having an affair and wanted a divorce. They had been married only two years!

Ted immediately scrambled for words and options and ideas that could bring restoration to their marriage. It had been good—once—hadn't it? How could busyness, lack of attention, or simple hard work be strong enough to destroy the love they had shared since college? Patty said it was "over." She considered it too late to reconcile their relationship because she was already planning to marry the other man.

Ted was physically sick. The reality of being in a failing marriage caused colitis and weight loss. People at work noticed, but he tried to keep his pending divorce a secret. He was certain that he could pull it back together. He had *always* been able to handle anything. But this situation—being a counselor who was unaware of his own wife's apparent unhappiness and infidelity—was more humiliation than he could bear.

He begged Patty to go to counseling with him. They went together. They went separately. They tried psychologists, psychiatrists, and marriage counselors. The advice they received ranged from "accepting the divorce" to "trying an open marriage"—which meant living together, but sleeping with others.

Ted could not emotionally handle those options. He had assumed *throughout his whole life* that he would be married only once. He had fully expected that the person he married would fill his deepest longing to be known and loved by another.

Though he had been raised in an Italian Catholic home, by the time he had reached his own conclusions about God, he had become an agnostic. He considered the rules and rituals of his childhood religion to be irrelevant to his life during his teens and twenties. He had no need for a religion that required ritualistic attendance, doing penance, or submitting to the advice of a group of robed clergy.

With nowhere else to turn, his shattered relationship and personal failure compelled him to search deeper for relief from the pain, guilt, and shame that he was carrying inside. He could not accept that his closest relationship had been stripped away from him. The emotional agony of divorce, the unsettling fact that no counselor could help them reconcile, plus the loss of most of his material possessions left Ted with one last option: to attempt to counsel himself.

Sitting on the floor of his once shared bedroom, Ted propped up pillows against the wall; his bed was already gone as part of the settlement. He grabbed the spiral notepad next to him and began to journal. He carried on a conversation with himself, much like a counselor would with a counselee. He openly expressed his remorse, pain, anger, and uncontrollable feelings. There was nothing to lose. There was nowhere else to turn. The person he had loved the most had walked out the door, never to return, planning to marry another. He had never experienced such great pain in his life.

Subtly, through the process of journaling, his mind opened up to the possibility that there was hope. He longed for a hope to hold on to. Then the thought came, *I have Someone to love you, Ted, and Someone for you to love.*

"Thank God," he whispered aloud. Then almost like a

voice in his head, he heard the words, *That's right, Ted. Thank God. I am here. I love you. You are not alone.*

Ted had never before, not for a moment, thought of God as Someone with whom he could have a relationship. He had not been shown or taught or even been open to know God in that form or manner. The knowledge that God was present, loving him, filling his heart with hope, relieving the depth of his pain, brought immediate peace to Ted's soul. He recognized that something, or perhaps Some*one*, had entered his room and body and mind and had spoken words of love and hope to him. Within hours and then days, the hope turned into a relationship with a living, loving God.

God filled Ted's emptiness by meeting his need for a deep love relationship. Upon the acknowledgment that God was real, Ted was immersed in the presence and power of God. He was given strength to face the inevitable divorce and courage to admit his own part in the broken marriage. Ted found the living, loving God—and not a religion—to heal his heart and help him get to the other side of his painful journey.

At that juncture, Ted found God to be a friend, counselor, and healer. Twenty-five years later, he continues to know and love God as his friend, counselor, healer, and more.

HE IS THERE; HE CARES

It was not through a church program or a planned religious event or a spiritual occasion that I found faith. Like many people of my generation, I had learned much about God and a particular denomination as a child, but I did not connect with what I had learned, or relate to it as a teenager or young adult.

When, at twenty-one, I truly looked for and sought to find God, it was through a stranger, the janitor, that I was introduced to Him as a Person who is holy and all-knowing, but loving and alive. I could grasp that concept of God, and it instantly connected me to my childhood pictures and lessons of Jesus Christ. The merger of my childhood faith with adult needs of my body, mind, and spirit was immediately compatible. What had been missing all throughout my teen and adult years—which had been present in my childhood—was the personal relationship I could have with God.

When God is explained to children, the easiest and most identifiable picture that is given is the person of Jesus as a shepherd, carpenter, and fisherman. He is described as a Person who lived and died for them, who was crucified on a cross and buried in a tomb, and as recorded and seen by witnesses, who was resurrected from the grave and ascended into heaven where He lives today. Children can understand and relate to such a person. They intuitively know that only Someone who loves them would be willing to die for them.

Somewhere in junior high these same children are drilled with creeds, commands, and catechisms and often completely forget that faith is a relationship with a living, loving God!

By adulthood, everybody has an opinion about God.

(Even no opinion is a statement in itself.) Some (the atheists) say, "There is no God." Others claim that God is everywhere, in everything. And theists believe that God is personal, that He exists. They believe that He created us and that He lives. Most unique to their view is that He *loves*.

GOD IS LOVE

An integral, foundational, not whimsical or fluffy belief about the God of the Bible is that He is a deeply compassionate, caring, and loving God.

One of the verses most often read or quoted from the Bible is John 3:16, "For God so loved the world that he gave his one and only Son, that whoever believes in him shall not perish but have eternal life." This verse articulates that the motive behind God's desire to be in a relationship with men and women throughout history is love.

■ ■ ■

Being seized by the power of a great affection is a life-changing occurrence.

■ ■ ■

God's passionate love for individuals is unfathomable. This intimate love cannot be duplicated in one's lifetime by any other experience or person. It has no bounds. It does not fade. It is not based on conditions or limits. And it is and was freely given to and for us before we even acknowledged it.

In reading *The Ragamuffin Gospel,* written by a former

priest, Brennan Manning, I came across a wonderful illustration:

> Over a hundred years ago in the Deep South, a phrase so common in our Christian culture today, "born again," was seldom or never used. Rather, the phrase used to describe the breakthrough into a personal relationship with Jesus Christ was, "I was seized by the power of a great affection."
>
> These words describe both the initiative of God and the explosion within the heart when Jesus, instead of being a face on a holy card with long hair and a robe with many folds, becomes real, alive, and Lord of one's personal and professional life.

Being seized by the power of a great affection is a perfect explanation of the life-changing experience that occurs when we enter into a personal relationship with God. It imparts new beginnings, hopes, perspectives, and plans into a previously confused, incomplete, or meaningless life. It has a physical and emotional sensation of being in a love relationship! It is not simply being in partnership with God; it is becoming a child of God as well as a part of the family of God!

7

A
ℛELATIONAL
FAITH . . .

INCLUDES BEING PART
OF A FAMILY

I'LL NEVER FORGET my first thoughts when I finished praying with the janitor. I looked up and actually wondered if my new acquaintance and I were the only two people on earth—at least that I knew of—who had experienced the presence and power of God! My next thought was to immediately make a mental list of all the people I wanted to tell about my encounter with God!

First of all, I wanted to share the sheer excitement I had about being loved by God, and then what it felt like to be given a second chance to live, with everyone who had seen me struggling. Then I wanted *all of them* to share in this new relationship with me. I reasoned that God certainly wasn't wanting to exclude anyone from knowing Him; therefore, I felt that if I just told people how wonderful and personal He was, they surely would want to know Him!

■ ■ ■

I wanted to share the sheer excitement I had about being loved by God.

■ ■ ■

The janitor broke my speeding thoughts with an invitation. He said that there was a family who lived on Third Avenue, only three blocks from me. He called them "believers." He told me that I was now part of the family of God, "united in fellowship" with them because they, too, were part of the family!

I was relieved that Ralph and I weren't the only ones who knew God! But where were all these believers? He told me that there were millions of people before and after me who called God their Father; who called Jesus their Savior, Lord, and Brother; and who had received the Holy Spirit to live within them as a sign and seal of their relationship with God throughout eternity! I just hadn't met most of them—yet!

Within hours, I was sitting at a kitchen table on Third Avenue with people I had never met before, but I honestly did not *feel* like a stranger to or around them. I felt like a long-lost member of a family who had been waiting expectantly for me to come home!

Each day I met more members of my new family—and I focused my energy on bringing "new kids" home with me!

It didn't stop there! I was so elated, so changed, so filled with love and gratitude toward God that I daily continued (and continue) to tell others about the relationship they can have with God that instantly makes them part of the family!

WE ARE THE FAMILY OF GOD

For many people of my generation who struggle to accept and understand faith, the image of God and the Father-child concept have undoubtedly caused some confusion and misunderstanding. For the many who have grown up in divorced homes without dads, or with fathers who were absent from their lives due to the demands of work, or with parents who "checked out of their lives" because of the use of drugs or alcohol, or who themselves were abused as children and then abused their own children, they find it very difficult to trust a Father they cannot see.

But there is a difference between the earthly family and the family of God. People who possess faith in the God of the Bible have a heavenly Father. They are called children of God and are ushered into a Father-child relationship with Him, *but without* the barriers of human-parental relationships, such as busyness, divorce, rejection, favoritism, and/or dysfunction.

Perhaps that is why in America the word *god* is more comfortably discussed as an idea or religion rather than a relationship. Maybe having a relationship with God, who is called "our Father," is terrifying to those who have already been disappointed, wounded, abandoned, or rejected by their fathers. When we possess faith in the God of the Bible, we enter into a dynamic relationship with a Father who—from before all time—loved us, planned for us, provides for us, and even disciplines us so that we might become all that we were meant to be!

For myself, being a child and grandchild of alcoholics, I was thrilled by—rather than afraid of—my new Father-child relationship with God! I wanted it. I needed it. I had been actively looking for a father's love in all of the wrong places prior to developing a personal relationship with God. Upon finding faith, I realized I had found my heavenly Father— who was unconditional in His love, always available and present, all-knowing, and all-powerful to help me with my many problems. And He was patiently waiting for me to willingly enter into this relationship with Him!

A. W. Tozer said, "What I believe about God is the most important thing about me." Relating to God as a Father who loved me allowed me to view myself as someone with value and purpose. This also gave me a new way of relating to others!

Let me assure you, discovering that I had inherited— become a part of—a new family, the family of God, certainly had its challenges. I learned quickly that I was required to treat other people equally, rather than differently. I found it a natural response to respect my elders, or those in authority over me. This was new and unexpected, and I can't say that I was prepared for it, but I did welcome the provision, protection, and safety within these relationships. In addition, I had to change the way I talked with, looked at, and spoke about others. Why? I truly respected the wisdom and faith that I was gleaning from my new family members.

■　■　■

Ultimately, in the family of God, we are all connected to each other, and yet individually and personally related to our Father in heaven.

■　■　■

But, as with any family, there are always those who mess things up for everybody, giving the whole family a bad name or reputation. Then there are those who make you so very proud to be related to them! Gratefully, in the family of God there are those who are older and wiser and willingly mentor those who are younger. And as in every family, there are the young ones who remind the older ones not to get lazy or lose their enthusiasm, purpose, or passion!

Ultimately, in the family of God, we are all connected to each other, and yet individually and personally related to our Father in heaven, who has no grandchildren. Our access to Him begins the day we call to Him. He promises never to leave us. He is never too busy to talk with us or listen to us. He is not a created idol or image to be worshiped. He is a living, loving God and Father, who created His children with the intention of communicating with them!

8

A
ℛELATIONAL
FAITH . . .

MAKES TALKING TO GOD
POSSIBLE!

My FIRST INSTINCT, on August 26, 1976, when the janitor told me that God . . .

- loved me,
- had a plan for my life,
- forgave me, and
- would help me overcome my addictions,

was to talk to God. If I had once held the belief or had the impression that a person couldn't talk directly *to* God or that some people weren't spiritual enough to talk *with* Him, I quickly overcame that misconception on the day that I asked Him to come into my life. My burning passion was to talk *directly* to God.

The first words I spoke to Him were straight from my heart, phrased from my own manner of speaking, and void of any lofty liturgical words or memorized prayers I had learned as a child. I immediately sensed that prayer was simply talking to God in a way that was normal and comfortable.

Without any reservations, I expressed every feeling to Him that I had been holding in for years. I confessed the guilt I was carrying inside because of my shameful behavior. I blurted out to God that I was embarrassed and ashamed and that I hated my lifestyle of unbridled drug abuse, alcohol use, and sexual activity. Yet, through all of my disclosure, I had complete confidence that God was not going to reject me for my honesty. I sensed that He understood my frailty and truly desired to help me with my problems.

The janitor did not give me spiritual guidelines about prayer, yet words unabashedly poured out of my heart and mouth to Him. And even though my problems were overwhelming and humiliating, they didn't stop me from talking to God. With childlike faith, I simply believed that God and I could communicate, even though I couldn't see Him.

I believe—and have experienced—that communication with God is *real*. I suggest to you that a relational faith is not based only on the amount of knowledge we have about God or our ability to articulate that knowledge, but it is a total "heart, mind, and body" encounter with the living, loving God that includes the interchange of conversation, emotion, and touch!

■ ■ ■

Communication with God is *real*.

■ ■ ■

I believe that God has provided—from before all time—tangible ways for human beings to be in contact with Him. We can speak to Him the way we speak to ANYONE—by verbally expressing or writing every thought or concern we have, and He speaks to us through His Word, His Son, and His creation.

Because I had once viewed prayer as strictly rehearsed, rote, memorized, or prewritten monologues for the spiritually elite, I was relieved to discover it to be more like a passionate, meditative, thought-provoking, honest dialogue between two people who shared a mutual love and commitment toward each other. In my passion to know God better, I have found a few ideas that have assured my successful communication with Him.

IDEA #1: JOURNAL OR WRITE YOUR PRAYERS.

In 1984, after I had been in a personal relationship with God for eight years, I found myself growing discontented with faith. It had almost become like a job or, even worse, a burden. This was particularly embarrassing because I was working for a Christian youth organization at the time. Not wanting to be a person who said faith was "everything," yet personally experiencing it to be irrelevant to my daily life, I began a personal search for what could have gone awry in what once was a very dynamic facet of my life.

By taking a closer look at the more practical aspects of my faith, I discovered that my dissatisfaction was not a matter of disbelief, but a distance in my relationship with God. Over time, I had simply allowed everything else—work, friendships, workouts, television, and extra sleep—to get in the way of my previously open, honest, intimate, and *daily* communication with God. Though it happened subtly, I had grown too busy or too tired to spend time with God. My attempts at speaking to Him (by spending time alone praying and meditating) or listening to Him (by quieting my heart and mind or by reading the Bible) had become sporadic and practiced only when convenient. After eliminating all the possibilities, I narrowed it down to lack of time with God that was creating my lack of enthusiasm about God and faith! The bottom line: faith had become an isolated compartment of my life rather than the center or hub of my existence.

Having read and heard so much about spiritual growth, I knew *intellectually* that certain spiritual disciplines, such as prayer, fasting, meditating, and Bible reading, were considered by all the "fathers of faith" as important and beneficial to maintaining a healthy spirituality, but my energetic, sanguine personality could not seem to *master* those disciplines! Once I understood that my longing for their benefits—such as supernatural power, insight, guidance, and hope—was strong enough to overcome my laziness after God, I was determined to find a way to achieve them.

After much internal deliberation, I merged my desires and my priorities, and in February of 1984, I made a very practical and purposeful decision to communicate daily with God. Because I considered time spent with Him to be more important and more valuable than any other hour in my day, I chose to make and keep a daily one-hour "appointment" with Him, even putting it on my calendar. In order to make this appointment a *two-way* conversation rather than a monologue, I combined the spiritual disciplines of talking to God with listening to Him speak.

To successfully avoid daydreaming, falling asleep, or being distracted from concentrating during this hour, I made the experience both practical and powerful by writing down my thoughts during those conversations. (This idea of written prayer was certainly not new. The book of Psalms includes written prayers, poems, and songs that fully express the hearts and hopes of those who penned them!)

Without fail, for the past thirteen years, I have recorded my words and God's responses in a three-ring binder called *My Partner Prayer Notebook,* which has been a visual place for me to "meet" with God. To quickly get past God's invisibility, when I put my pen to the paper, I picture or imagine that I am writing to *or* speaking with Him *and* that He is listening to me and will respond to me! In addition to providing a tangible resource for me to express all of these thoughts, hopes, dreams, and confessions to God, the method of journaling prayer has provided the accountability and excitement that I need to *keep* my appointment with God.

Over these years, this pattern for spending time with God has remained simple enough to not become cumbersome, visual enough to keep my appointment with God exciting, and yet detailed and disciplined enough to guide me through stages of growth and maturity in knowing God. Most important, I have more than 4,500 hours of recorded conversations with God, not only my words to Him, but His responses to me! Written prayer has been the key to keeping my faith from becoming a compartment in my life and remaining a relationship with God.

IDEA #2: MAKE AN APPOINTMENT WITH GOD.

Only when I made it one of my highest priorities to have a daily appointment with God did I fully understand how much He loved me and wanted to reveal Himself to me. As in any relationship that is a priority, planned time together always enhances trust, love, and honesty. I found that spending time with God was no different. By *making* my appointment with God a *nonnegotiable* hour of my day, I have been successful to keep that appointment. I've also been realistic enough to know that I would have to accommodate for the many changes that would inevitably come with each season of my life as well as my ever-changing marital, parental, and occupational responsibilities.

I believe the key to my success is that I plan for my appointment with God *one day in advance.* No two days are the same in every week, and because I don't want to set myself up for failure, I look at tomorrow's lineup of responsibilities and roles (mother, wife, boss, etc.) and schedule my time with God during the first uninterrupted hour in my day. I refer to this particular hour in my day as my "quiet time." I feel most connected to God during this time—whether I am at the kitchen table, out in the yard on a lawn chair, or by the fireplace. I actually assume that He is beside me or with me.

■   ■   ■

By *making* my appointment with God a *nonnegotiable* hour of my day, I have been successful to keep that appointment.

■   ■   ■

Because the God of the Bible is a triune God—Father, Son, and Holy Spirit—I picture Jesus as the person of God who is talking, listening, encouraging, correcting, and spending time with me. When I see Jesus as the actual Person I am communicating with, I am not struggling to connect with a mystical, magical, angelic image of a god. I am communicating with a Person. And though His physical appearance and apparel might lack detail, the mental picture that I have of Him is of a gentle shepherd, a hardworking carpenter, a teacher, and a man who liked to fish with His friends. By referring to the image of Jesus as a shepherd, carpenter, teacher, or fisherman, I am extremely comfortable and never threatened during my hour appointment with Him. In those minutes, I am freely communicating with a kind, gentle, powerful friend and Father rather than a kingly, unapproachable ruler.

Equally important, I believe that God communicates directly with me. In fact, I am daily encouraged to continue having conversations with God because of the continuous signs, responses, and answers I have received to my prayers. I have a God who communicates with me, takes any "religion" out of my devotion to God, and replaces it with a relationship!

IDEA #3: DAILY ADMIT YOUR SHORTCOMINGS TO GOD.

I really think that the Twelve-Step groups (AA, NA, OA, etc.) have a corner on the market when it comes to admission, confession, and forgiveness. Making it a daily practice (Step 10) to rid your mind of guilt, doubt, and a poor self-concept by confessing any known sin (such as any unforgiveness, resentment, outbursts of anger, secret jealousies, or even hate) is the ultimate way to make friends and influence people. I believe that it greatly enhances the personality and character of men and women to take a "daily inventory" of themselves—shortcomings and all—and ask for God's help to change.

If we reasonably conclude that all people have failed,

made mistakes, struggled with selfishness, impure motives, and anger . . . then talking to God about these flaws is a non-threatening place to begin the difficult process of change! Taking the time and having the courage to take a daily inventory of where you have fallen short and where you need to make restitution or attempt reconciliation *can only improve* your interpersonal relationships and personal self-esteem.

There are simple and complex ways to go about this. I actually have an "Admit" section in my prayer time notebook. It is obviously not public record, but it is a personal confession of the areas that I need and want to change in my life. Some people consider the practice of confession as taking an inventory. Others simply call it "identifying their issues."

I use a portion of Scripture, found in Psalm 139:23–24, to help me begin my daily search! These verses ask God to search my heart for any habits, patterns, or offensive ways that are either visible or hiding in my life, but that will harm me or others. Then I ask Him to *change* those ways about me. Every day—some days spent in this section are more intense than others—I have an opportunity to honestly and openly talk with God about the areas that are going wrong in my life and my personality, and I ask Him to help me change.

This is always interesting. Some days are tougher than other days. Some days are more of a victory than other days. Some days, I can feel as if I have a long way to go, and on other days, I feel as if I've come a long way!

Most wonderful, though, is my perception of God's love toward me. I am convinced that His love doesn't waver, nor is it based on my performance. I have depended upon a promise and principle in 1 John 1:9: "If we confess our sins, he is faithful and just and will forgive us our sins and purify us from all unrighteousness."

I have come to understand that He is not forgiving because I *deserve* it, because I have earned it, or even because I am sorry. But it is His *unchanging* nature to forgive the repentant, *willing-to-change* sinner.

This phenomenon—God's forgiveness toward me and His power to change me—brings me back to this journal section *every* day. I am never so afraid or ashamed that I *can't* come to a holy God, but I am very grateful that He is so merciful, compassionate, willing, and powerful to help me change!

Perhaps this type of unconditional love and forgiveness is not presently available in the majority of your relationships. When you enter into a personal relationship with God, it is promised. In fact, Romans 8:38–39 says that *nothing*, not "death nor life, neither angels nor demons, neither the present nor the future, nor any powers, neither height nor depth, nor anything else in all creation," can separate us from God's love!

As in anything that sounds too good to be true, if tested over time, the truth is revealed. I am personally convinced that the practice of daily confessing my shortcomings to God, especially in writing, has freed me from the dark habits and negative thinking that have consistently tried to hinder and hold me back from being all that I was meant to be!

■ ■ ■

The practice of daily confessing my shortcomings
to God has freed me from dark habits and
negative thinking.

■ ■ ■

IDEA #4: KEEP A WRITTEN LIST OF PEOPLE FOR WHOM TO PRAY.

For mainly practical reasons, I suggest that you keep a running, written prayer list. First, praying for others is a very positive, powerful way to care for others and the outcome of their situations. It is a very unselfish, other-centered act of your will and heart and mind. In addition, it takes time, involves commitment, and actually increases your love for another.

Second, having a great memory is the luxury of a select few. If you don't want to forget to talk to God about the needs and desires of others, then you'll have to write them down!

Third, keeping a written record of *what* you have asked God to do is also proof positive that He answers prayers! In twenty years, I have not found God to be at all reluctant in His answers to prayer; in fact, He is overwhelmingly generous. But in addition to saying "yes" answers to my prayers, God says, "No," "Not right now," and "Not in that way, but in this way . . ."

When you make a written list of specific requests to

God, then watch, wait, and see how He chooses to answer, it serves as an incredible boost to your faith and provides personal proof that there is a God who answers prayer!

Last year, my friend asked me to pray for her during a trip that she would be taking to war-torn Bosnia. Though the threat of danger was imminent, she was committed to going to that country as an ambassador of an international Christian service organization. She gave me the specific dates when she would be gone, October 14–21, and several times before she left, she reminded me to pray for her safety.

During that very week, (1) my father went into the hospital with congestive heart failure, (2) I was in the process of writing a book, and (3) my travel schedule was particularly full. Had I not written down her specific request or the dates that she would be gone, I honestly don't think that I would have remembered to pray for her. But because her detailed request was a part of my daily prayer list, I prayed for her. I could identify with the fact that as a wife and mom, her life being in danger was not only personally unsettling but also had a huge effect on her family, as well. Therefore, with great diligence, though my own life was extremely full, I would go through my prayer list, and upon seeing her name, I would talk with God about her safety and mission in Bosnia.

On October 18, I awoke at thirteen minutes after midnight. I sat up in bed, not wondering why I was awake. I knew instinctively that I needed to pray for Dale until the urge subsided. I awoke from a sound sleep one more time that night and prayed fervently for Dale's safety. At 8:30 A.M., when my assistant came into the office, I felt compelled to ask her to join me in prayer for Dale's safety. Then one more time before lunch, I was stopped midstream in my busy routine and prompted to pray for Dale.

Dale had told me that she would be returning to her office on October 21. I called her East Coast office as soon as I got up that morning. When I told her when and how I had been compelled to pray for her, she told me her story. She verified that each time I had been urged to pray for her in *my* time zone on October 18 was the only day in *that* time zone that her party was in danger. As I listened by phone, I was amazed at how their extensive struggle with a flat tire on a very dangerous road in Bosnia lined up with the times that I had been awakened or prompted to pray for her.

We could not explain my sensitivity to pray for her, but we were both grateful that we were two people who believed in the power of prayer. From a more practical viewpoint, I was certain that without my written prayer list, I would not have been acutely aware of my friend's need for intervening prayer!

IDEA #5: GET RID OF ANY MISCONCEPTIONS YOU MIGHT HAVE ABOUT PRAYER.

For more than five years, I have spent many weekends away from home motivating people to pray. I am compelled to do this, I believe, because I have found that prayer—a two-way conversation with God—is the most exciting, powerful, dynamic, and relational aspect of knowing God. I simply want to share my greatest "find" with others. Those who know me can attest that I would not personally be involved with or solicitous about something that is tedious, fruitless, or lacking in excitement! Yet, in my travels, I have found the greatest deterrents to prayer are the many misconceptions about it!

Over the past twelve years, written prayer has proven to me that God answers prayer, but in many different ways. I have merged those experiences and answers with the advice and illustrations found in the Bible to help wipe out any misconceptions that might hinder someone from experiencing a relational faith!

■ Misconception #1: It's Not Okay to Ask.

If you've ever been told that . . .

- God is too busy,
- certain requests are too insignificant, or
- to pray for yourself is selfish,

now would be an ideal time to take a short course in what the Bible says about "asking" God for help, advice, or intervention. After accumulating all the verses that I could find containing the words *ask* and *pray,* I was overwhelmed by the discovery that "it's okay to ask!" I'm not proposing or promising that you'll receive the answers you wanted or hoped for, but a principle that is repeated over and over in the Bible is "ask."

Asking doesn't mean telling. Asking doesn't mean demanding. Asking is an appeal, a petition, a bid, an inquiry.

O. Hallesby, author of *Prayer,* said, "When God says 'yes,' it is because He loves us. And when God says 'no,' it is because He loves us." This simple principle encourages me to think of God as a Father who is never too busy or never too late with an answer, who is understanding of my humanity, and who desires the best for me—whether it comes in the form of correction or comfort. After twenty years of "asking" God in prayer, I am still learning that He will answer prayer in His time and with an answer that will be the best for all those involved. And after twenty years of "asking" God in prayer, I am personally and absolutely convinced that "it's okay to ask!"

∎ ∎ ∎

I am still learning that He will answer prayer in His time and with an answer that will be the best for all those involved.

∎ ∎ ∎

∎ Misconception #2: You Shouldn't Pray About Something Too Often, Too Hard, or Too Much!

From all the research I've accumulated about those throughout the centuries who have communicated with God, there was and is one consistent thread: persevere in prayer! The perseverance principle was often the common denominator for those who received the most unusual and extraordinary answers to prayer! These men and women of

God were especially tenacious to hang on and wait for God to intervene when they had only the hope and confidence that God had spoken to them, or they felt that He had given them specific direction and plans to follow. When the going got tough, they held on to their vision, idea, conviction, or dream by continually talking to God about it.

The troubles, roadblocks, disappointments, and mountains that spring up, trying to keep us from reaching our goals, are common to all men and women. It is in those trials that prayer is the vehicle that allows faith to persevere and not give up. It is the fuel of courage. And in those times when the circumstances don't validate our hope or give us proof, communicating with *the God who planned for us, loves us, and communicates with us* will be the only asset we have to hold on to, to believe what we can't see!

Prayer is an action step that sustains *our* faith in the waiting and pleases God. Whether we like it or not, *perseverance* in prayer—trusting, hanging on, discussing and identifying our fears, asking for direction—is essential to a relational faith.

■ *Misconception #3: Prayer Is a Boring "Time Waster."*

I think a common misconception about prayer, meditation, fasting, and Bible reading is that these "disciplines of the spiritual life" are often considered liturgical, boring, or a waste of time. I can say that because I once had that perspective of prayer!

When I was young, I thought prayer was for the elderly

or the clergy! When I grew older, I considered the "spiritual disciplines" as tedious time wasters that accomplished very little. When I became convinced that I was actually missing out on something, I set aside one hour a day with God, and EVERYTHING in my life got exciting, moved at a fast pace, changed, erupted, split wide open, and became adventurous! Now, I can't name anything in my life that produces *more* exciting results than prayer, meditating, fasting, and Bible reading!

I have found that talking with God is the action step that fuels a dream, turning it from hope into reality. It is the spark that sets and keeps my heart on fire to fulfill my purpose! Prayer gives me stamina over the "long haul." It reminds me not to forget from "whence" I came! It is talking *and* listening to the Creator, Architect, and Author of my life!

In any given situation, at any moment in time, for any problem, in any location, anyone who calls upon the God of the Bible *will be heard.*

I cannot validate what is released through

- yoga,
- mantras,
- visualization, or
- New Age meditation,

but I can verify that two-way conversations with God WILL release His power in your life, most specifically because I have volumes of handwritten pages where I have recorded how God has answered specific prayer requests through words read during my daily Bible reading, which instructed me or helped me make a decision. I am personally convinced that God absolutely speaks to and listens to those He knows and loves, simply because I have tested the theory!

■ ■ ■

I can verify that two-way conversations with God WILL release His power in your life.

■ ■ ■

One skeptic who attended my prayer workshop left ready to disprove my assertions. She made a list of 130 prayer requests and spoke to God each day for one month about each of them. She contacted me at the end of the thirty days to tell me that God had answered 127 of them specifically! Though she didn't tell me *how* God answered each specific request, she knew that He had met her and worked in each situation.

I can't tell you how God will respond to you, but I can tell you how He has responded to me and to those in the Bible. I can't promise that the moment you talk to Him, you'll be relieved of your suffering. You may simply be sustained through it.

I can't tell you what or how or when God is going to work and move and intervene, but if and when *you* begin to communicate with Him in transparent, genuine two-way conversation, I believe that you *will* experience His presence, receive His answers, find comfort and rescue for your situation.

I have found that communicating with God—not just talking to Him, but also listening—is the most accessible action step that a believer has in order to elicit change in his or her life!

A

ℛELATIONAL

FAITH . . .

MAKES LISTENING TO GOD
POSSIBLE!

H AVE YOU EVER wondered if hearing God's voice was only for the prophets in the Bible? Or if God did speak, what His voice would sound like? Have you ever wondered if you have heard God's voice?

A great hindrance to many who ponder faith is the mystery of trying to communicate with Someone you can't actually see. Perhaps that is why when I talk with God, I write out my conversations with Him, and when I listen to Him, I use the Bible, His written Word, as my main source for hearing His voice speak directly to me. But in addition to the Bible, I hear Him speak to me through His creation (both the world around me and those in it), His Son, and His Spirit.

I am the type who needs to see to understand. I am

satisfied only if I get solid answers to my questions. I don't give up searching for an answer very easily. In fact, my visual, impulsive learning style made it much more difficult for me to become a spiritual person. But once I understood that God could—*and wanted to*—communicate with me, show me the way to go, light my path through a variety of tangible resources, it took the uncertainty out of being able to know and communicate with God and gave me great assurance that He was always there!

GOD SPEAKS THROUGH HIS WORD, THE BIBLE

Though following the Bible's morals and values as a way of life is not easy by anyone's standards, I have found security and stability within its directives because its tenets have not changed over time. And even in the situations where a decision has to be made that is difficult, unusual, or confusing, I still find that the Word of God contains basic principles on which I can rely.

The Bible is *more* than a book of history or a list of "do's and don'ts." It is meant to be the source of God's voice to His children. When it is read with the intention of receiving *His* counsel, viewpoint, reasoning, and truths, its words become a stable, unchanging resource by which to judge and evaluate our past, present, and future.

■   ■   ■

The Bible is God's voice to His children.

■   ■   ■

Theologian and teacher A. W. Tozer put it succinctly, "God did not write a book and send it by messenger to be read at a distance by unaided minds. He spoke a book and lives in His spoken words, constantly speaking His words and causing the power of them to persist across the years."

The Bible itself is a unique vehicle for communication because it is able to speak to, teach, and inspire any reader from any generation, in any circumstance or location, on *how* to be in relationship with the Creator as well as with all that is created. In addition, it provides historical documentation of God's relationship with human beings throughout recorded time as revealed through the documentaries of His followers. The Bible is not only a history book but also a guidebook on how to live the life of faith. It provides vital information about how much He loves us and longs to be in a relationship with us.

The Word of God, in the form of the Bible, was given to human beings with the condition that it would remain unchangeable with the times or trends of each generation or culture. By disclosing moral absolutes to us, God has been able to strongly, purposefully, wisely, and justly speak to each person's conscience and heart with a "voice" that provides guidelines for living that are not subject to pressure or popularity.

Through the life illustrations detailed in the Bible, God

is able to use these people as role models to give us direction and advice for our future. Through illustrations of hope for recovery and healing, the Bible imparts hope to the hurting much like a loving Father, counselor, or friend would who was right there with us. What the Bible proposes as precepts by which we can live in harmony with other people and all of creation are not religious dogmas or political agendas, but the wisely crafted words of our Creator.

Yes, the Bible is the written history of our relationship with God. In simple language, it provides answers regarding God's existence, His creation, our fallen nature, and God's solution for our reconciliation to Him through Jesus' crucifixion, resurrection, and ascension.

It is the answer book for people with questions.

It is the voice of God to man.

It is more than good ideas, great thinking, or unproven theory.

It is God's words, spoken and recorded.

The Bible's uniqueness and simplicity lie in its blend of historical record, poetry, parables, law, and eyewitness accounts. It . . .

flows like a time line,

reads like short stories that interrelate,

captures the common emotions of every

human being, and

provides answers for our deepest

questions.

If we believe that the Bible has been inspired by an infinite, personal Creator *who intimately knows us* with all our limits and who has created us in His own image, not only can we view the Bible as God's personal instruction to us, but we can get to know God better through the life of Jesus Christ, so vividly detailed within its pages.

God's Word, like His Son, was *given* so that all men and women—without regard to their economic class, religious denomination, culture, creed, or color—might hear His voice and understand His love. To God's people, the Bible is His *written* Word. Jesus, God's Son, is the living, *incarnate* Word. Therefore, *any man or woman* can find and know God as well as hear Him speak through His written Word, the Bible, and through the life and testimony of His Son, Jesus.

GOD SPEAKS THROUGH THE LIFE OF JESUS

The Bible clearly has a central and most controversial focus: Jesus. In the Old Testament, Jesus is concealed, but foretold as the Son of God who would come to earth as the Messiah. In the New Testament, He is revealed, rules, and reigns as God's only means of reconciliation with man. Therefore, the Bible speaks to every generation who came before and after Jesus Christ of the opportunity to be in a relationship with God, the Father and Creator.

Blaise Pascal, the great French mathematician and physicist in the 1600s, was one of the most influential men to explain to the skeptics of his time the dynamic opportunity a person has to communicate with God. Boldly, he discussed his beliefs in the *Pensées:*

> We know God only through Jesus Christ. Without this mediator, all communication with God is broken off. Through Jesus we know God. All those who have claimed to know God and prove his existence without Jesus Christ have only had futile proofs to offer. But to prove Christ, we have the prophecies which are solid and palpable proofs. By being fulfilled and proved true by the event, these prophecies show that these truths are certain and thus prove that Jesus is divine. In him and through him, therefore, we know God. Apart from that, without Scripture, without original sin, without the necessary mediator, who was promised and came, it is impossible to prove absolutely that God exists, or to teach sound doctrine and sound morality. But through and in Christ we can prove God's existence, and teach both doctrine and morality. Therefore Jesus is the true God of men.

In his mind, it was "not only impossible, but useless to know God without Christ."

■ ■ ■

God is attainable by anyone who acknowledges the person of Jesus Christ was God in time and history.

■ ■ ■

Pascal spoke to the scholar and to the uneducated alike, arguing that to know God is not unreachable for anyone, but attainable by anyone who acknowledges the person of Jesus

Christ was God in time and history. Jesus was called the living, incarnate Word. We can know of Him by reading about Him in the Word. We can know Him personally by entering into a relationship with Him by faith!

GOD SPEAKS THROUGH HIS CREATION

God speaks visibly through His creation—which is neither an audible nor a written word, but the visual expression of who He is. It is His art. In the color of the sky, in the formation of the clouds, or in the temperature and temperament of the sea or air, God the Creator is communicating to and with His creation in ways that no person or machine can control, program, or fabricate.

To explain the origin and creation of the deserts, fertile land, sea, or mountains throughout the history of time would be a most difficult, arduous and, perhaps for most of us, impossible task. But what we can all agree upon is that the design, imagination, integration, and weaving of all creation were and are beyond one *man's* ability or comprehension. Though I am not a scientist or geologist, I cannot rationally assume that the creation of the universe was a mere accident. I find it much more logical to conclude that the creation of this intricately contrived world—and all that lives within it—was possible only at the hands of a master Creator. I find security, safety, and order within that belief.

But does this creation *speak* for God? The first impression we receive when observing our surroundings, not through a microscope or telescope but with our eyes, is the awesome beauty that is displayed in the sky, mountains, bodies of water, plants, flowers, and trees. The vivid and muted colors, the variety of forms and substances, and the individuality of each insect, animal, and person speak volumes of their Designer. Creation whispers *and* thunders limitless illustrations of God's intimacy, creativity, power, and detail.

Throughout all time, there has been no machine or man (besides Jesus) or nation that has stopped the sky from raining, the winds from twisting into hurricanes, or the earth from quaking. The uniqueness of creation is that it is both incredibly beautiful and unfathomably forceful. Though every created person has an innate ability to create, no man or woman could presume to repeat, interrupt, design, or bring into existence by his or her limited imagination the unlimited complexity of creation.

■ ■ ■

Creation whispers *and* thunders limitless illustrations of God's intimacy, creativity, power, and detail.

■ ■ ■

Thus, the purpose and power of creation are undeniably visible and impact the life of every person. They determine where we settle, how we survive, what we invent, what resources we use, and how well we relate to each other and all other facets of creation, including our Creator.

God's artwork—His creation—is both the voice and the hand of God communicating to His people.

LISTENING ELICITS CHANGE!

Perhaps the greatest evidence that people have listened to and heard God's voice—even more significant than being able to articulate their knowledge of God or confirming their membership in a denomination or religion—is that those words have changed them! Those who have truly heard God speak to them through His Word, His Son, or His creation can't help but be changed. They understand much better who they are. They realize that they have been created with a desire *to know God*. They are aware that what they *do* is a reflection of what they *believe*—and who they *know*.

Incredibly significant to a relational faith is the understanding that men and women are not puppets, slaves, or servants. We are related to God and His family as well as able to communicate with Him.

Faith that is relational is *not* a religion, a complex set of rules, a state of mind, an idea, or an "it." Faith that is relational is entering into the deepest love relationship that one can ever know, have, or experience. A relational faith believes that God does exist. A relational faith is the response of one individual accepting, trusting, and believing in a living, loving God who cares for and communicates with him or her! Faith is being seized by love.

10

A

RADICAL

FAITH . . .

CHANGES HEARTS AND MINDS!

THROUGHOUT THIS BOOK, I have shared the stories of people—Peter, Candice, Ted, and me—whose lives were changed by the transforming power of faith. Yet, there are two more people, friends of mine—a speech therapist and a thirty-five-year-old man in real estate—who in their own words relate the stories of how a radical faith changed their lives. Once they considered faith foolish, the Bible rubbish, the rules of religion tedious. When they discovered that faith was radical, based on truth that they could believe in their hearts, they too experienced the transforming power of faith that changed their lives. I share their stories with you to encourage you to believe that faith can change *your* life, as well.

KINNEY'S STORY

When I woke up in a strange bed on that snowy morning, I knew that everything I had known in my ten and a half years of life would be changed forever. The night before, December 8, our furnace had exploded, and my childhood home burned to the ground. Miraculously, I had crawled on my belly down the steps in order to get out, and I had been rescued just in time. My darling four-and-a-half-year-old sister, Katie, had not been so fortunate. Apparently, in the confusion of smoke and flame, she became trapped in her closet, thinking it was the way out, and she was asphyxiated by the fumes and smoke.

When I fell into a fretful sleep at our neighbors' home, the night before, I hoped against hope that Katie had survived, but it was not to be. She died in the fire. I never said "good-bye," never got to tell her how much I loved her, never got to see her again. My older sister and my mother had miraculously survived the fire, as did my father, who was out of town on business when our tragedy occurred, but our Katie, the best one of all of us, was gone.

After the fire, we chose to follow the counsel of, "Put a smile on your face, be a brick, and go through life as if nothing had ever happened." We never talked about the fire, but on its anniversary every year, as on Katie's birthday, our home would have a heaviness in the air that no one discussed. Spiritually, we were not led to God since my parents weren't interested in worshiping any God who would let their Katie die. They had not known Him well enough before the fire to receive comfort, love, and grace from Him after it. They could only justify turning away from an unknown God, who had ruined their lives.

My method of coping with my unresolved grief was to become a clown. Of all my achievements while growing up, I was most proud to have been named "class comedian" by my fellow students. Between getting strokes for being funny and numbing all my very REAL painful thoughts through alcohol abuse, I deceived myself into thinking, *This is about as good as it gets!*

By the time I was twenty-three years old, I was living an entirely inauthentic, fragile, performance-based existence, and my nerves were shot. Mostly due to "survivor guilt" and unresolved grief, I went through therapy for anxiety and depression. If you saw the movie *Ordinary People,* with Timothy Hutton, Mary Tyler Moore, and Judd Hirsch, you may remember the scene where Hirsch, a psychiatrist, said to Hutton, a teenage boy who had survived a boating accident that killed his brother, "What did you do that was so terrible?" Hutton passionately cried out, "I didn't die!" That was my dilemma, too. I masked my troubled spirit by holding a very responsible job as a speech pathologist. As long as people loved my work, or loved me FOR my work, I was okay.

About that time, another event occurred that forever changed the course of my life. While out bowling with some friends, I looked across the smoke-filled bar and saw a very dashing young man looking at me. As our eyes met, I said to myself, "I'm going to marry him." I was shocked by my own thoughts because I had never felt that way before about anyone, especially having just laid eyes on the man.

The attraction was quickly mutual, and we had a fairytale romance for a month before my new love got a job out of state. As the months wore on and our relationship grew through our long-distance courtship, I had only one *red flag* about the man of my dreams: he was a born-again Christian. Unfortunately, I despised people who identified themselves with Jesus Christ. I thought they were all nerdy wimps, and there was no way that my true love was going to be one of them.

I set out to rescue my boyfriend from Jesus by undertaking to read the Bible and prove to him that it was totally foolish and wrong. Little did I know that my plan would completely backfire. As I read the first three Gospels, I said smugly, "These are nice fables, but that's all they really are." It was reading the book of John that "did me in." As I read the words, "For God so loved the world that he gave his one and only Son, that whoever believes in him shall not perish but have eternal life," I whispered to myself, "This God cares about people. He actually has FEELINGS . . . like love. He seems alive."

I tried to dismiss those thoughts, and I continued my crusade to rescue my future husband from all that foolishness. But by the time I read through John and got to chapter 14, something very serious had happened to me. I will never forget the words of John 14:6, which almost jumped off the page at me, where Jesus talks about Himself and says, "I am the way and the truth and the life. No one comes to the Father except through me." As I read those powerful words, my heart was pounding. "Jesus is saying that He is the way to God," I whispered to my newly awakened self. "He LOVES me. He loves me even though I have hated Him and mocked Him and tried to get my boyfriend away from Him."

I lay on my face on the floor of my bedroom and cried out to God . . . for the first time in my fragile life. I asked God to forgive me for all my sin. I told Him I believed Jesus WAS the way to Him, and I even said that I recognized that Jesus was absolutely God. I began to understand that God loved me enough to draw me to His Word so that I could be truly rescued from death, this time through receiving eternal life by acknowledging that Jesus' death on the cross was in my place.

I was in awe that in spite of my mockery, disbelief, and even hatred of Him, He still chose to reach into my scarred and wounded heart to bring me healing and new life. It has been a twenty-year journey with Jesus to date, filled with miracle after miracle.

Thirty-four years after the fire, I no longer dread the anniversary of that horrible event. Now I joyfully celebrate the birthday of my precious daughter, who was given to my husband—that dashing young man from the bowling alley— and me in a miraculous act of love. Our daughter's birth mother, in reading the anonymous resume we had written as prospective adoptive parents, said, "I will know I am to give my child to this woman if God gives me a baby girl on December 8, the date that her sister died in their fire." He did, and she did . . . and that's our child. Four months later, God grew a normal, healthy sister for our first child in my totally infertile body. Our lives are not perfect, just free, forgiven, and eternally with Jesus.

WAYNE'S STORY

Growing up in Newport Beach, California, I was exposed to every possible distraction from God, and I took advantage of those situations for the pursuit of pleasure. Although I had gone to Sunday school a couple of times at a Protestant church, and I believed in an all-powerful God, I had no idea about the significance of Jesus. I saw church as a stifling, boring place, only for the socially inept "sticks-in-the-mud," and by the time I was in high school, I found much more fun and excitement in the world of "sex, drugs, and rock and roll."

My involvement with the party life and its bedfellows became more entrenched in my life during college, and I shunned those who dared to approach me about the attributes of a godly lifestyle. Surrounded by wealth and opportunity, I was determined to be "self-made." I was certain that I didn't need God!

As a young professional in sales, I would say and do anything for a buck, convinced that is the way in which men are measured. My identity became my paychecks, my cars, and the women I dated. Unfortunately, those things never seemed to be enough. I consistently jumped from one job to another, bought new and better cars, and also flowed through a string of failed relationships in search of "something." But I had no idea *what* that "something" was that I was looking for.

After two very tough years of working in the commercial real estate market in southern California, my little self-made empire began to crumble. I could no longer afford my ocean-view condo or my five-hundred-dollar-a-month convertible car payment. My relationships with my family and girlfriend were strained because I was working fifteen-hour days with little or no paycheck. My identity, even my *manhood,* was in jeopardy.

Knowing my financial condition would not improve soon, I began considering changes. Within two weeks, I had given my share (my debt) of the condo to my partner and quit my job. I even sold my car to a guy who stopped me on the street and asked if I would consider selling it. And yes, my girlfriend was gone by then as well. All I had left was my mountain bike, a borrowed VW camper van, and lots of time.

Being an adventurous type, I decided to take a short mountain biking trip up the coast for a couple of weeks. Traveling lightly, I took along two books I had recently received for my birthday from my old girlfriend: a Bible and Josh McDowell's *Evidence That Demands a Verdict.* I determined to read the entire Bible, just as I would read any other historical literature, beginning with the first page, Genesis 1:1.

Two months later I traveled to a small town in the Cascade mountain range of Washington. My life consisted of mountain biking, living in my van, and waiting tables on weekends. By then, I was well into the Bible, and I had many questions about it when I overheard another waiter telling the cooks about heaven and hell. Soon, he and I began to meet for breakfast to discuss grace, mercy, and God's forgiveness. He would answer the questions I had each week, then I'd go along my way, traveling throughout Washington and British Columbia, reading more. At one meeting he simply told me to take the knowledge about God that was in my head and put it in my heart. He encouraged me to say the "sinner's prayer" and ask Jesus to come into my life.

On my next road trip, I was heading up into the mountains when my van overheated, and I had to leave it alongside the road. I hitchhiked until I wound up in the back of a bitter-cold, icy pickup truck. It was then that I decided I needed help. I succumbed to the idea that I couldn't do "it" alone anymore. I admitted right then that I needed God! While lying on my back, looking up at the snow-covered trees hurtling by me at sixty miles per hour, I said the simple prayer the waiter had suggested. I'll never forget that moment. Although freezing cold, I was warmed by the idea of a new beginning.

I remained at my mountain retreat for another month before the cold became intolerable. At that point, I moved into the basement of my Christian friend's house for a couple of weeks, and I read more books about faith, such as Josh McDowell's *More Than a Carpenter,* and even attended Bible studies with his friends. I prayed to be released from the temptations I faced, and I was most amazed by God's power and ability to change me!

I returned to southern California and began a serious quest for a better understanding of God's precepts and His plan for my new life. I had finally found what was missing in my life, and I could truly say that all my past triumphs paled in comparison to the peace and joy I had found in a relationship with Jesus Christ. As an immediate result, I built positive relationships with men and women at a church in my town. In addition, I found myself giving of my spare time and musical gifts to the youth ministry. In the process, I met and married the most godly, beautiful woman you could ever imagine.

Looking back, I believe God had been trying very hard to reach me and to reveal His love and plan for me. I just wouldn't let Him get through my layers of worldly desires and personal sin. When I lost everything, He allowed me to get to a point where I would listen. In that loneliness and silence, I found God.

I most identify with author Henri Nouwen, who wrote, "Solitude is the furnace of transformation." Indeed, my life has changed!

11

A
ℛADICAL
FAITH . . .

MAKES BOLD CLAIMS!

Nℴℴ EVERYONE HAS the need to intellectually ponder the claims of faith.

But I contend that people who will set their minds to discovering the truth about the Bible and claims of Jesus Christ *will find answers* in which they can place their faith. I find it most interesting that intelligent people will reject or, worse, ignore faith in the God of the Bible without even researching its claims for themselves! I would strongly encourage any person, whether you consider your faith strong, weak, or nonexistent, to personally search out the claims of the God of the Bible and the faith He calls us to. In fact, I suggest that you use the same tests and parameters that you have set for considering true the writings of Socrates, the history of ancient Rome, or the historical accounts of other famous figures of the past!

Within the innumerable volumes of history, facts, and

documents available to any seeker lie the very data that satisfy the intellect and convince the mind that faith is not
blindly believing, but believing in proven evidence about a
God we cannot see! In fact, I have studied and researched
many of the authors and scholars who have written about
faith and have included them in the bibliography of this
book. But in my own motivational style, I have narrowed a
radical faith down to seven BOLD CLAIMS.

CLAIM #1: THE WORD OF GOD IS TRUTH.

Up until the age of twenty-one, I considered the Bible
to be a token leather book one receives upon completing
religious confirmation classes! I changed my mind about that
leather book when I became desperate enough to search for,
look for, even grasp for something or someone outside
myself to change and help me. It was only then that I understood that the Bible was God's Word, and if I wanted to get
to know God better, I needed to read it! At twenty-one, I
discovered the Bible as the revelation or disclosure of the living, loving God. I saw the Bible as the tool He could use to
relate to every man and woman! From that point to the present, I have considered the Bible to be my greatest single
guidebook for living a good life—in feeling good, reaping
good, and knowing how to be good!

In wanting to know God—and myself—better, I have
found the Bible to be an extremely multifaceted, readily
available resource. Not only does it serve to answer tough

questions, but it is a constant source of inspiration, strength, direction, and power. In addition, it is the place to which I can always turn for repeated reminders that I am a loved child of God!

Many argue that there are other books with equal ability to influence one's life. Billy Graham, one of the greatest evangelists of the twentieth century, believes,

> The Bible easily qualifies as the only Book in which is God's revelation. There are many bibles of different religions; there is the Muslim Koran, the Buddhist Canon of Sacred Scripture, the Zoroastrian Zend-Avesta, and the Brahman Vedas. Anyone can read them, comparing them to the Bible, and judge for themselves. It is soon discovered that all these non-Christian bibles have *parts of truth* in them, but they are all developments ultimately in the wrong direction. They all begin with some flashes of true light, and end in utter darkness. Even the most casual observer soon discovers that the Bible is radically different. It is the only Book that offers man a redemption and points the way out of his dilemmas. It is our one sure guide in an unsure world.

My personal experience in reading the Bible almost daily for more than twenty years is that it provides me with *continual* revelation. I am daily being enlightened, taught, encouraged, comforted, corrected, and filled with hope by reading and adhering to the tenets of the faith as taught in the Bible. I am directed and motivated by its time-proven truths and absolutes, such as the Ten Commandments. And I am increasingly filled with love for God and others by reading the psalms, songs, poems, and prayers that other men and women of faith have recorded within its pages.

In an article entitled "More Than Great Literature," Billy Graham, one of the most highly respected Americans of all time (having just received the Congressional Gold Medal in 1996, the highest honor that Congress can bestow upon a citizen), additionally describes the Bible:

> Sixteen hundred years were needed to complete the writing of the Bible. It is the work of more than thirty authors, each of whom acted as a scribe of God. Those men, many of whom lived generations apart, did not set down merely what they thought or hoped. They acted as channels for God's revelation; they wrote as He directed them; and under His divine inspiration they were able to see the great and enduring truths, and to record them that other men might see and know them too.
>
> During these sixteen hundred years, the sixty-six books of the Bible were written by men of different languages, living in different times, and in different countries; but the message they wrote was one.
>
> When the great scholars gathered together the many ancient manuscripts written in Hebrew, Aramaic and Greek, and translated them into a single modern tongue, they found that God's promises remained unchanged, His great message to man had not varied.

In this one book people can find answers to life's most difficult questions: where they have come from, how they are to live in the present, and what their future holds.

When the Bible is approached as true and applied to our

lives as truth, the result of God's revelation to us is peace, power, and purpose.

CLAIM #2: THE WORD OF GOD IS REAL, NOT ROMANTIC.

A radical faith believes that the Bible is not a romantic ideal, but a Book whose accounts and claims are real.

Francis Schaeffer was an intellectual and spiritual author of the twentieth century who wrote twenty-three books on Christian thinking and faith. The L'Abri Fellowship, which he founded with his wife in 1955, was a learning place that branched into Switzerland, Holland, Sweden, and the U.S., where he boldly taught and defended the Bible as God's absolute truth.

From his book *No Little People,* I appreciated his view of the Bible:

> If someone asked us, "What is the Bible?" we probably would not begin our answer by saying, "The Bible is a realistic book." Yet in the twentieth century this might be the best place to start—to stress the realism of the Bible in contrast to the romanticism which characterizes the twentieth-century concept of religion. To most modern people, truth is to be sought through some sort of leap from which we extract our own personal religious experiences.

> Many feel that the Bible should portray a romantic view of life, but the Bible is actually the most realistic book in the world. It does not glibly say, "God's in His heaven—all's right

with the world!" It faces the world's dilemmas squarely. Yet, unlike modern *realism* which ends in despair, it has answers for the dilemmas.

So when we say that the Bible is a realistic book, this is not just a theoretical proposition on a metaphysical chessboard. It relates to realities in life—realities in the home, in government, in the way we look at the world.

I personally believe that one of the greatest discoveries—and possessions—that people receive when they enter into a personal relationship with God is the Bible. Detailed and woven through the lives, experiences, patterns, principles, and promises in every book and chapter of the Bible is God's viewpoint on how to live with and love others, yourself, and God. Throughout the Bible, we find that God doesn't hide Himself from us. He reveals Himself to us, then asks us to trust and rely on Him.

For the believer, the Bible takes conjecture out of living the life of faith and replaces it with certainty. That is the very reason I do not avoid referring to the Bible when I defend my faith. It is a solid, historical, practical, proven record that God is and always has been intimately involved in the lives of those He created, cares for, and communicates with! In fact, I have found no other book—and there are about five hundred on the bookshelves of my home and office—that is so real and so relevant to my life as a woman, spouse, mother, and communicator!

▪ ▪ ▪

For the believer, the Bible takes conjecture out of living the life of faith and replaces it with certainty.

▪ ▪ ▪

CLAIM #3: IT PROVIDES AN UNCHANGING MORAL CODE FOR PEOPLE—BECAUSE THEY NEED IT!

I find it astonishing that the Ten Commandments have been taken out of the classrooms of American public schools, but they are being added to the former Soviet Union classrooms! I am utterly amazed that our nation does *not* want to promote the Judeo-Christian morals, yet a nation (formerly the USSR) subjected to seventy-three years of godlessness and communism is desperately seeking moral teaching for its students!

What does this reaction imply about our country? How can Americans be so afraid of time-proven guidelines for moral living? Perhaps it is too threatening to a society that is heralded for its liberal ideals and laziness toward duty, respect, honesty, and purity to be asked to consider morality as an esteemed goal? Perhaps words such as *honor* and *sacrifice* have become too demanding? Maybe today's leaders no longer want to push— or be pushed—toward higher standards? These are questions a moral code answers for men, women, and country.

C. S. Lewis, whom *Time* magazine described as "one

of the most influential spokesmen for Christianity in the English-speaking world," said, "Morals are directions for running the human machine." The Bible clearly states that there are physical, spiritual, *and* moral laws in the universe. It goes so far as to give the details of its origination—the places, times, and people to whom these laws were given. And they were clearly and specifically not man-made laws, but laws based upon and derived from the very character of God. Yes, they were called "commands." And from before the beginning of recorded time, these commands—God's commands—contained absolutes that defined right from wrong as well as differentiated good from evil.

Hence, it logically follows that if someone chooses to violate, ignore, or break any of those commands or absolutes, he or she is really choosing to rebel against God. It also follows that those who rebel against Him expose themselves to predetermined consequences that will inevitably lead to personal moral breakdown. Parents know this pattern as "breaking the rules" and "suffering the consequences," though not all parents can uphold their rules or handle the rebellion of their children! God defines this rebellion as sin, which sadly results in separation between man and God, or man and others.

Have you noticed how the word *sin* raises the tone and temperature of a conversation when it is discussed? Why is *sin* such a harsh and threatening word in our culture? And why is it considered too presumptuous of a holy God to give standards, design rules, or set boundaries that have predetermined consequences attached to them? Perhaps the true question is, "Could all men and women live in peace and harmony without a written moral code to guide them?"

Throughout history, we have proven that we are not pure enough in motive or character to be each other's peacemakers, authoritarians, or judges. Our perception is limited and finite, our motives are skewed selfishly, and our track record over time speaks for itself! Only the Bible, because it is based on the character and absolutes of a holy God, is able to purely and justly give moral standards and answers to men and women by which to live.

If the Bible is considered true in teaching and precept for every generation, it would follow that it should elicit a response from those who read it. As a society, many Americans have opted to ignore and even ridicule the unchanging morals and values of their Judeo-Christian heritage that are found in the Bible. Instead of referring to the Ten Commandments or the Golden Rule as truth by which men and women of all races can live (which only up until forty years ago were posted in most American public school classrooms), we have resorted to judging life by the standards or values that each individual has deemed personally significant or satisfying. Needless to say, even without detailed documentation, I believe that our nation has approached such moral decay that kids killing kids and carrying guns is the "norm" rather than an appalling, unacceptable way of life. Without respect for the teaching in the Bible, we have become a nation where lust and selfishness have replaced goodness and love.

I don't need to judge this observation by anyone else's

life. I only need to look as far as my own life to be certain that not a lack of, but a rejection of, moral teaching was the cause of my demise. By letting self-fulfillment drive my life, I immediately gauged all my decisions and choices by what *felt* good to me rather than a code of ethics centered in truth and morality.

I actually remember living off the self-talk popular in the seventies that continually reminded me that only *I* mattered. Within a few short years, the results of that self-counsel proved to completely bankrupt me physically, mentally, financially, and emotionally.

Then to what do I attribute my revised change in attitude, action, and focus? It was not a guru, an organization, or another popular seventies cure—a mantra. With great sincerity, I am personally convinced that I would not be free of drugs and alcohol, married, and deeply committed to one man for nineteen years, the parent of a great young man, *or even alive* had I not let the moral teachings of the Bible influence my life for the last twenty years. I believe that the time-tested set of moral laws that I had been taught as a child, but only as an adult determined to live by, is the teaching that changed my life in 1976 and has afforded me a wonderful quality of life ever since.

CLAIM #4: THE BIBLE IS AUTHENTIC.

There are many who would argue that the Bible is full of inconsistencies and error. I have discovered otherwise. In fact, in my own investigation of the authenticity of the Bible, I found several authors who had originally considered the Bible to be unreliable, but because of their own findings became convinced of its authenticity.

Charles Colson, a lawyer and politician, wrote that "the men who penned the New Testament were Hebrews, and scholars agree that the Hebrews were meticulous in precise and literal transcriptions. What was said or done had to be recorded in painstaking and faithful detail; if there was any doubt on a particular event or detail, it was not included."

In *Loving God,* Charles Colson discussed how he approached believing in the Bible as a document that could be defended and proven. He concluded that the external evidence about the Bible "continues to add historical verification. New archeological discoveries in the field of biblical studies have added weight to the evidence that the Gospels were written by contemporaries of Jesus." He added that "critical historical issues are not all neatly resolved, of course, and probably never will be. Yet it is an underreported fact that the more evidence is uncovered, the more scholars agree (even those who don't consider Jesus deity) that the New Testament is a reliable accounting of what the writers saw and heard."

If people want to be convinced scientifically and intellectually of the validity of the Bible, they only need to begin to examine the scrupulous and extensive research that has been made by authors such as C. S. Lewis, Francis Schaeffer, and Josh McDowell. Within the volumes that these men have written, there are substantial critical, documented investigation and examination of the Bible's authenticity that stand up against and compare to other historical documents.

For example, in *Evidence That Demands a Verdict,* Josh McDowell documents historical evidences that defend and define the Bible's truth and authenticity as well as validate Jesus' claim to be the only Son of God. As a matter of scholarship, he used scientific and historical approaches to his examination of the Bible and the life of Jesus. His team of researchers consisted of colleagues from Michigan, Ohio, and Bowling Green State Universities, as well as those from Louisiana Tech and Virginia Polytechnic Universities. Throughout his books, he confirms the reliability of the Bible as historical text by using archaeological tests. He dissects the claims of Jesus Christ as God's Son, the Messiah prophesied, and verifies the historical documentation of the Resurrection. I consider his books to be some of the most valuable tools to which I can refer those who have any doubts or uncertainty that the Bible is true and Jesus was who He said He was—God.

Granted, not every individual who encounters faith has to be convinced that the Bible is an authentic, historical document, but for those who need or want that proof, it is available! And once they have satisfied *their* standards for deeming the Bible authentic, they gain confidence and trust that come from studying, reading, teaching from, and following the tenets of a document that has been scientifically tested for its validity—historically, chronologically, and geographically.

Even more important, they can believe with abandon in a time-tested, nonchanging, and nonnegotiable document!

CLAIM #5: JESUS WAS GOD IN THE FLESH.

In the book *God Came Near,* a beloved storyteller of our generation, Max Lucado, describes the obvious absurdities of Jesus' life on earth that have proceeded to frustrate people throughout the ages. He writes,

> You mean to tell me God became a baby and that he was born in a sheep stable? And then after becoming a baby, he was raised in a blue-collar home? He never wrote any books or held any offices, yet he called himself the Son of God? He never traveled outside of his own country, never studied at a university, never lived in a palace, and yet asked to be regarded as the creator of the universe? And this crucifixion story . . . he was betrayed by his own people? No followers came to his defense? And then he was executed . . . buried in a grave . . . and according to what's written, after three days in the grave he was resurrected and made appearances to over five hundred people?

A faith that is radical believes exactly these things—it believes, in short, that *Jesus was God . . .*

- who came to earth in the flesh,
- died on a cross for the sins of all mankind,
- was buried and raised from the dead after three days, and
- appeared to eyewitnesses before ascending into heaven.

99

Those who believe that Jesus was God's Son and came to earth in the flesh are not unintelligent, whimsical religious fanatics. They are more often people who have considered the incredible amount of factual and scientific documentation regarding the facts of Jesus' life, death, and resurrection and have become convinced by their findings that they can intellectually *place their faith in the fact* that Jesus was God.

In Charles Colson's propositional research of the Bible, he concluded that an

> infallible God cannot err; a holy God cannot deceive; a perfect teacher cannot be mistaken. So He is either telling the truth, or He is not who He says He is. Therefore, if Christ's divinity and perfect humanity are established, we know that His view of Scriptures as infallible and authoritative is true. The real proof of the Scripture's authenticity, then turns on the proof of Christ's authenticity.

As a lawyer looking for a key to breaking the circular argument and proof of Christ's authenticity, Colson wrote, "It is the fact that He was bodily raised from the grave. The historical truth of His victory over death and His consequent eternal kingship over the world affirms Jesus' claim to be God. The Resurrection establishes Christ's authority and thus validates His teachings about the Bible and Himself."

More specifically, there are several hundred, but sixty-one major, predictions foretelling God's Son, which were recorded in the Old Testament and written hundreds of years before Jesus was born. He fulfilled these prophecies, and they have been documented in the New Testament!

In Josh McDowell and Bill Wilson's book, *A Ready Defense,* is a quote by Professor Thomas Arnold, author of the three-volume *History of Rome,* who was holder of the chair of modern history at Oxford. Professor Arnold said,

> I have been used for many years to study the histories of other times and to examine and weigh the evidence of those who have written about them, and I know of no one fact in the history of mankind which is proved by better and fuller evidence of every sort, to the understanding of a fair inquirer, than the great sign which God hath given us that Christ died and rose again from the dead.

Also noted in *A Ready Defense* was another reference to the resurrection of Christ by English scholar Brooke Foss Wescott, who said, "Taking all the evidence together, it is not too much to say that there is no historic incident better or more variously supported than the resurrection of Christ."

All of the prophecies recorded and predicted in the Old and New Testaments about the life, death, and resurrection of God's Son were fulfilled in the person of Jesus Christ. To those who thought He was God, He claimed to be the Son of God, sent to earth by God to reconcile all men unto His Father.

Of the sixty-one major prophecies *that Jesus fulfilled,* the probability that this could be mere coincidence was ruled out by Peter Stoner in *Science Speaks.* He calculated that if even eight of the prophecies were fulfilled, using the science of probability, the chance that one man might have fulfilled all eight of them is one in 10 to the 17th.

If you were to debate that the prophecies were not given by God's divine inspiration, you would have just one chance in 10 to the 17th of having them come true in *any* man, yet they all came true in Christ! Stoner found that "the fulfillment of these eight prophecies alone proves that God inspired the writing of those prophecies to a definiteness which lacks only one chance in 10 to the 17th of being absolute!"

I find it impossible to argue with statistics and studies like the ones above. For me to believe that Jesus came in the flesh is not as difficult as it would be for me to doubt His documented presence on earth.

CLAIM #6: JESUS DIED ON A CROSS AND ROSE THREE DAYS LATER FROM THE GRAVE.

Of all the major religions of the world, only four present their followers with a personality as their leader. Of the Jews, Muslims, and Buddhists, none believe that their founders came back to life after they died. Thus, the resurrection of Jesus Christ is a major tenet of a radical faith. To believe only that He was a good prophet is to miss the most fundamental aspect of Jesus' work on earth. He died on a cross. He rose from the dead. He foretold His resurrection. His tomb was found empty, though soldiers had stood guard throughout the night. And it was historically documented that more than five hundred people saw Him after His resurrection from death.

A radical faith believes in the historical resurrection of Jesus Christ and, therefore, is able to believe and trust in the words He spoke, the lessons He taught, the promises He made, and the miracles He performed.

■ ■ ■

A radical faith believes in the historical resurrection of Jesus Christ and, therefore, is able to believe and trust in the words He spoke, the lessons He taught, the promises He made, and the miracles He performed.

■ ■ ■

When I understood—and personalized—the purpose of the Cross and Resurrection, I understood—and personalized—that God loved me. When I took time to comprehend Jesus' sacrifice unto death, I was overwhelmed by God's love for me. My response to that love was to place my faith in Jesus because it cost Him *everything* to reconcile me to a holy God. Only then did I understand the Crucifixion and Resurrection as acts of God's love toward me, not simply Christian holidays.

In *Whatever Happened to the Human Race?* Francis Schaeffer wrote,

The Resurrection of Christ is presented in the Gospels as verifiable history. It is given in the same frame of reference as applies in science—when Christ arose, He did not leave His body in the grave. The Resurrection was open to normal observation. There were the graveclothes. Jesus spoke to the disciples. He could be touched. He ate before them.

If Jesus did not live, or if He did not rise from the dead, Christianity cannot continue. It cannot live on as a mere *idea,* because Christianity is about objective truth and not merely religious experiences. Both the Old Testament and the New Testament claim to be truth, in contrast to that which is not true, and this truth is rooted in history. We have only one hope, and it rests on a serious commitment to the existence of God and the reliability of His Word, the Bible, in all the areas in which it speaks.

Either Christ rose from the dead as an objective fact of history, or He did not. If He did not, Christianity is finished.

CLAIM #7: HE LIVES!

That He . . .

- left His grave clothes in the tomb,
- appeared to Mary Magdalene and to the women who were leaving the tomb,
- broke a Roman seal (which meant the stone over the tomb had to be rolled away, even though it took an entire Roman guard to seal the tomb), and
- silenced His critics, without any refutation of His resurrection . . .

only begins to form the evidence that causes me to believe in the resurrection of Jesus Christ. That Christ appeared to a variety of people over a period of time that included varied reactions and situations adds credibility that these testimonies were not fabricated by a small group of individuals in the same place or moment in time. In addition, once their claims were recorded and published, there were still people alive who could have refuted the testimony of those eyewitnesses, but did not.

Perhaps the greatest claim a radical faith makes is that God exists, Christ lives, and His Holy Spirit dwells within those of us who call Him our God!

The power of every person's indisputable experience with the living God validates his relationship with Him. It is his or her reality. Each person's story of how he encountered God provides another poignant illustration to those observing his life that God does exist. Just as the specific details of how I met my spouse describe to others how my life changed direction when I met someone significant, so my description of knowing God is my record of our relationship. My experience with God is not a figment of my imagination but an explanation of my encounter with Someone who has physically, emotionally, and spiritually changed my life.

I often have the opportunity to tell old friends and new acquaintances about my experiences with God. In fact, my faith is most easily explained and almost always well received when I simply share about my relationship with God. Whether I tell about my troubled life before I encountered God (in my twenties) and how dramatically I changed once God came into my life, or more currently about how I sensed God's presence during my dad's final week of life on earth, my *personal experience* with God is often more acceptable to an unbeliever or skeptic than any historical facts and evidences that I could rattle off.

When people share their experience of transformation, crediting the living, loving God with their visible, tangible change, this validates faith and allows others to hope, search, and find that God is powerful, present, and personal in our time.

■ ■ ■

My *personal experience* with God is often more acceptable to an unbeliever or skeptic than any historical facts and evidences that I could rattle off.

■ ■ ■

Most often, I have found that it is not knowledge that people lack about God that makes faith elusive, but it is an experience *with* God that is missing in their lives.

12

A

$\mathscr{R}$ADICAL

FAITH . . .

SOMETIMES CREATES
TENSION!

IN AMERICA, DURING the 1950s and 1960s, people generally classified themselves as Protestant or Catholic, religious or Christian or Jewish. Those labels were very normal and acceptable—then. Now, in the 1990s, though it has occurred gradually over my lifetime, I often find myself in the minority as a follower and lover of God. If the subject of Christianity or Jesus is brought up, I genuinely feel a "God" tension. Even phrases such as "Praise the Lord," "Thank You, Jesus," and "You must be born again," are often considered repulsive, threatening, or intimidating wording, rather than perceived as expressions of love and enthusiasm toward or about the God who *is* love.

Almost everywhere I turn, angry, rude words and the sometimes hostile attitudes and actions of people confirm that they are not followers, much less lovers, of God. I get frustrated when I think that people are disinterested in, even refuse to consider, having a personal relationship with God because of their misconceptions about Him, unanswered scientific questions, or a difficult religious situation or experience they had that unfortunately misrepresented Him and confused them.

I find this unapproachable attitude perplexing because I am almost certain that those who are rejecting the God of the Bible *are also* looking for a deep and unconditional love. I am equally convinced that they are not going to find this incredible kind of love anywhere other than through a personal relationship with God.

I'll never forget how, as a "new" believer, I boldly shared my experience of faith—which was evidenced in my abruptly changing life as well as through my use of actual Bible quotes that I had newly discovered—with anyone who would listen. My particular group of observers included the mechanics at the car dealership where I was employed at the time, my party buddies, and many of my relatives. Every one of them seemed surprised that I could speak so confidently, even knowledgeably, about the Bible and God, whom I had only recently discovered! They were both curious about and impressed with my newfound ability to debate and discuss my beliefs. Most of them were truly amazed that I suddenly possessed solid answers and strong opinions about many of life's dilemmas, inconsistencies, and concerns that only weeks earlier had been the source of my bitter complaints and despair.

What I experienced was common to every child of God who becomes a student of the Bible! God's viewpoints, which are found in the Bible, are accessible to any man or woman to read, believe, and ultimately follow. These new convictions, then, are not based on our own understanding or on another human being's ideas or found in an organizational creed or doctrine. They have been around for centuries!

Though I often frustrated and even angered those who didn't believe as I did, I did not waiver in my beliefs. Whether I was talking with my girlfriends who couldn't understand my not very trendy abstinence stands or with my coworkers who noticed the abrupt cleanup of my language, those who knew me before my encounter with faith also knew that I did not have a religious education that could have given me such instant knowledge or fortitude.

Unfortunately, in addition to their growing confusion and skepticism was an underlying irritation. They began to ask, "Who are you to be so outspoken with 'right or wrong' and tout abstinence, morality, and ethics?" And they questioned my conviction that there was only one way to God. Those discussions inevitably created tension in many of my relationships.

TENSION #1: A RADICAL FAITH REQUIRES TAKING STANDS AGAINST CULTURAL NORMS.

Within the first few months of entering into faith, I completely read through the entire Bible once as well as repeatedly listened to audiotapes of every book of the New Testament. No one asked me to do these things, though my janitor friend suggested that I learn more about the Bible. Because I was daily changing and improving in every facet of my life, I was actually looking for explanations and answers! I enthusiastically read the Bible to increase my knowledge and to satisfy my curiosity.

What I gained from this huge consumption of data was an understanding about life as seen through God's eyes. In contrast to my own views—or even my friends' or parents' views—I could not refute the power, pertinence, or purity that was described throughout the Bible. Thus, I became a self-taught student of the Bible. The result? I rapidly gained wisdom, knowledge, and conviction to view life from a very radical perspective—which was called faith!

I know that I am not alone here. Many people who come to faith, especially after a difficult struggle or previous stance of atheism or godlessness, often find the Bible to give them a new perspective for living. I have seen persons with very abrasive personalities abruptly turn into kind or generous people. I have watched adults who were living together, upon understanding God's viewpoint on marital fidelity, separate until marriage or simply split up. I have witnessed people with deeply rooted prejudices immediately let go of them and stand by the directives established in God's Word for dealing equally with all mankind. I have observed enemies—even family members—reconcile and embrace each other when confronted with God's viewpoint on forgiveness. Yes, faith *is* radical because it has the power to change a man's ingrained or inherent viewpoints about the world around him, especially when the world is moving in a different direction or at a different pace!

Unbelievably, God's viewpoints are the very values that our country now struggles with teaching its children. In the August 1996 United Airlines magazine called *Hemisphere,* I read an article about Michael Josephson's organization *Character Counts!* Though it is not a religious organization, he has been opposed by liberal organizations who don't want him to bring "religious principles" into public schools. That his *Six Pillars of Character*—trustworthiness, responsibility, respect, fairness, caring, and citizenship—happen to align with Judeo-Christian values apparently has created great concern and controversy. Josephson explained that as a lawyer and as a parent, he found that if we don't build character and values into young people, those qualities will atrophy.

It certainly is a different America in which I am raising my son from the one I was raised in during the fifties and sixties, and that my parents were raised in during the thirties and forties. In the past, our country upheld God as good and evil as wrong—even shameful! Today, the moral message is very confusing.

In America, godly values, the Ten Commandments, and moral character have been not only forgotten, but frighteningly hated. When a nation rejects morality, history shows that it should anticipate the decline and demise of its society. If the condition of our public schools is not enough indication that our nation is declining, then the increase in those schools of guns, pregnancies, abortions, gangs, dropouts, and substance abuse should speak loudly enough. Our nation's children have become statistics, lying in the morgues, the slain victims of a growingly godless society. Only those with a radical faith can and will stand against the cultural norms of a declining nation.

TENSION #2: A RADICAL FAITH REQUIRES REPENTANCE!

It was in my initial moments of embracing God and faith that I spoke the words "I am a sinner" for the first time. Contrary to the popular belief that such an admission could be humiliating, self-incriminating, or even permanently damaging, I found it to be one of the most freeing confessions of my life! In fact, I had not felt that guilt-free in years, as when I openly confessed to God in front of another person my shortcomings and failures.

Whether I had been fooling others or lying to myself, it was certainly no secret that I had been living an immoral, abusive, alcoholic life. The sheer energy that it took to hide much of my daily lifestyle was exhausting to me both emotionally and physically. Therefore, by the time I hit bottom—and my life was exposed to all for what it really was—admitting that I was a "sinner" was by far the least of my troubles. What I found most interesting was that, unlike people who could easily reject me or be repulsed by me, God was waiting for me.

In *The Faithful Christian,* an anthology of Billy Graham's life and writings, he says,

> God caused the Bible to be written for the express purpose of revealing to man God's plan for his redemption. God caused this Book to be written that He might make His everlasting laws clear to His children, and that they might have His great wisdom to guide them and His great love to comfort them as they make their way through life. For without the Bible, this world would indeed be a dark and frightening place, without signpost or beacon.

When I consider the Bible as confirmation, documentation, and record of God's love and light, I am overwhelmed with the thought that I have a living, loving God who *meant for me to know Him, understand Him, and recognize how He wanted to work in my life.*

- I am relieved of the frantic search for truth when I consider how God intentionally provided His words to guide, strengthen, and show me the way to live on earth (until we are together in heaven).

113

- I am motivated to love and serve God because He loved me enough to show me the way to Himself—through His Son. I have been given this truth in His Word.
- I am at peace with my future because I have been shown God's specific plan for redemption in the pages of the Bible. He made it clear. He made it available to all, to any!

I know of no document other than God's Word that can withstand the pressure of the much-heralded, feel-good, humanistic viewpoint that we are not born sinful. Not only do we struggle with the concept that we are sinful, but we find it impossible to admit that, as individuals, we are sinners who must turn from sin.

In differing degrees, at varying speeds, and in a myriad of methods all men and women fall short of a holy God. We can argue with that statement until the day we die, or we can face the fact that sin is common to all. Once that issue is no longer an issue, we can acknowledge our personal sin and our personal—rather than corporate or congregational—need for a Savior.

In *The Fundamentals,* Blaise Pascal, a sixteenth-century physicist, wrote,

> The Christian religion then teaches men these two truths: that there is a God whom men can know, and that there is a corruption in their nature which renders them unworthy of Him. It is equally important to men to know these points; and it is equally dangerous for man to know God without

knowing his own wretchedness, and to know his own wretchedness without knowing the Redeemer who can free him from it. The knowledge of only one of these points gives rise either to the pride of philosophers, who have known God, and not their own wretchedness, or to the despair of atheists who know their own wretchedness, but not the Redeemer.

His death and resurrection are historical facts, but more importantly the acts upon which man, who is separated from God because of sin, can be reconciled to a holy God. In simple words, man needed a Savior, whether he finds that easy or difficult to admit.

This is the dilemma for all of us. Will we admit to personal sin? If we will, we must accept that the next step is repentance—or sorrow—which leads to a changed heart toward a holy God. Depending upon our personality, upbringing, and personal pain, this step of repentance might take a lifetime. Yet, the earlier it is approached in one's life, the greater chance one has of possessing a faith that is deeply trusting, firmly rooted, and noticeably radical! (Research shows that 90 percent of those who have a personal relationship with God made that decision before they were eighteen years old.)

Charles Colson writes in *Loving God,*

Repentance is replete with radical implications, for a fundamental change of mind not only turns us from the sinful past, but transforms our life plan, values, ethics, and actions as we begin to see the world through God's eyes rather than ours. That kind of transformation requires the ultimate surrender of self.

The call to repentance—individual and corporate—is one of the most consistent themes of Scripture.

Though it is a most difficult task, and admittedly a huge tension, every person must confront the holiness of the living, loving God in light of his or her own sin.

■   ■   ■

Every person must confront the holiness of the living, loving God in light of his or her own sin.

■   ■   ■

TENSION #3: A RADICAL FAITH REQUIRES BELIEF THAT JESUS WAS GOD IN THE FLESH.

God does not ask us to guess, assume, or wish hard that He exists and that He sent His Son to earth in the flesh. We are not asked to slip into intellectual suicide with sheer abandon and pretend that we are not curious, logical, factual beings. We are not required to hold on to a blind hope that *maybe* Jesus was God and that *perhaps* we should believe that He was resurrected from the dead. But we are asked to make a decision about whether Jesus was God in the flesh based on the facts.

In my research, I read much about, and what has been

written by, a particular 1960s college student named Josh McDowell. It was said that he loved to have fun and held great parties, and he made a point of ridiculing those who called themselves Christians. (You might have met people like this.)

He was genuinely puzzled by peers who openly professed faith in Jesus Christ. He considered it incredulous that intelligent people could be so misguided. But a time came when he was challenged by his friends to stop ridiculing them until he had considered the claims of Christ:

- That He was God's Son,
- That He took on human flesh,
- That He lived on earth among real people,
- That He died on the cross for the sins of mankind,
- That He was buried, and
- That three days later He rose from the dead and appeared to eyewitnesses.

Out of pride, Josh finally accepted the challenge of his friends to refute the claims of Jesus Christ. After researching the evidence and the historical facts in order to prove that Jesus was a liar or a lunatic, he unexpectedly came to the conclusion that Jesus Christ must have been who He said He was—Lord. Though his findings proved to be a blow to his ego, he admitted that the Bible was true and that Jesus was Lord, and he began to pursue a personal relationship with God. The outcome of his research was the background information for two of his best-selling books, *More Than a Carpenter* and *Evidence That Demands a Verdict*. (If your heart and mind require more evidence, I strongly suggest that your research begin with McDowell's books!)

C. S. Lewis, the twentieth-century author and theologian, was another man who convinced many intellectual, but skeptical persons that the Bible was truth and Jesus was God in the flesh. In *Mere Christianity,* he wrote,

> I am trying here to prevent anyone from saying the really foolish thing that people often say about Him: "I'm ready to accept Jesus as a great moral teacher, but I don't accept His claim to be God." That is the one thing we must not say. A man who was merely a man and said the sort of things Jesus said would not be a great moral teacher. He would either be a lunatic—on a level with the man who says he is a poached egg—or else he would be the Devil of Hell. You must make your choice. Either this man was, and is, the Son of God: or else a madman or something worse. You can shut Him up for a fool, you can spit at Him and kill Him as a demon; or you can fall at His feet and call Him Lord and God. But let us not come with any patronizing nonsense about His being a great human teacher. He has not left that open to us. He did not intend to.

WE LIVE IN A RADICAL, CONTROVERSIAL DAY

In an age and era where faith is so controversial politically, socially, and intellectually, it is radical to believe that the

Bible is our source of truth and that Jesus Christ was God in the flesh. Charles Colson, in *Loving God,* writes, "Indeed, in a world where values are being shaped by the fleeting fantasies of secular humanism, it is *radical* to stand for the fundamental truth of God, to go to the root, the Word of God."

Colson is certainly right about my world! I do live in a time and nation where fact is fiction, right is wrong, and what is openly evil is considered good. That is why I *need* a radical faith that provides truth to live by and a Person—not an "it"—in whom I can place my trust. Indeed it is a radical faith that makes bold claims and sometimes creates tension, yet is able to stand against the tide of my world and the test of time.

■ ■ ■

It is a radical faith that makes bold claims and sometimes creates tension, yet is able to stand against the tide of my world and the test of time.

■ ■ ■

Beware. When you pursue a radical faith with all of your heart and soul and mind—it will absolutely revolutionize your life!

13

A

ℛEVOLUTIONARY

FAITH . . .

BRINGS CHANGE THAT
HAS A *GOOD* EFFECT!

T HOSE OF US who have been touched by God's love and immersed in His forgiveness toward us have a common way of overreacting! We no longer spend all of our free time with our old buddies. We monopolize most of our conversations with the details of our new relationship, and we possess the faraway look of someone who is infatuated or consumed by love. All of a sudden, we have become instant God-promoters, walking Bible-quoters, and joyful "praise the Lord-ers."

The motive behind what appears to be madness is actually the desire to give God credit and recognition for the obvious positive lifestyle changes that are occurring within us. Unashamedly, and almost desperately, we want to introduce everyone we know to God as a lover rather than an extremely distant "lawgiver" or fun killer. But very often, our zealousness makes things worse—at least initially.

TWENTY YEARS AGO . . .

Within days of being transformed by God's love, I so radically changed in my appearance, conversation, and actions that I quickly had very little in common with my friends. Unfortunately, we parted ways with much misunderstanding.

Also at that time, I was living with a man I thought I would eventually marry. I was in love with him, but our commitment to each other resembled the 1970s' loose-love, live-in style of that era.

The moment I asked God to come *into* my life, I felt that I should move *out* of the house we were sharing. My decision took my boyfriend off guard. He expressed a genuine concern for my emotional stability. He wondered if I had gone overboard. He questioned my need to publicly admit that I was an alcoholic. He voiced a strong opinion that God might be a crutch, which he thought only weak people needed.

I was torn. Perhaps I needed a crutch? Prior to my conversion to Christ, I *couldn't stop* drinking, swearing, doing drugs, or being involved sexually. No matter how self-destructive those habits became, they overpowered my will to quit. But immediately upon asking Christ to come into my life—and I mean within the hour—I stopped drinking, swearing, smoking, doing drugs, and having sex outside marriage. Inviting Christ to come into my life was a completely life-changing and mind-altering experience— though at first, only *I* saw these changes as good!

The extremely dramatic physical, emotional, and spiritual changes that occurred were so powerful and dominating that the love my boyfriend and I had once shared was simply not strong enough to hold us together through our differences. I can honestly admit that the most heartbreaking aspect of my newly possessed faith was that I could not persuade my boyfriend to love and accept the new me—or my God—and I had to let go of one of them in order to survive. I painfully chose to let go of my boyfriend.

This was a most critical point in my new relationship with God. I was being asked to make a very difficult choice, give up someone I truly loved and had been intimate with, *because of my faith*. I struggled emotionally with the potential loss of one love in order to hold on to the love of Someone I couldn't see. I regularly begged Kevin to consider the claims of Christ for himself and to share my faith, but he just could not do that for me or anyone. Daily, I dealt with much internal pain, rejection, and even self-pity. Yet I could not fathom returning to the lifestyle that had stolen my self-respect and came near to stealing my very life.

I cried myself to sleep nightly and finally realized that we were at an impasse. Only a new believer for two months, I relinquished my ability to change this situation, and I moved back to Ohio to pursue a path of following God and telling others about His love. My boyfriend remained in California.

Our lives drifted apart. We married others and completely lost track of each other.

TWENTY YEARS LATER . . .

While in Monterey, California, in 1995, I attended a lecture series by Dr. Earl Palmer of Seattle. My goal in attending the seminar was to gain a clearer understanding of how to effectively communicate the revolutionary phenomenon that occurs when one enters into a personal relationship with God! Though I had been to many lectures and heard hundreds of sermons over the past twenty years, I was looking for something profound, yet simple, to enlighten me. I was not disappointed.

Within the first few minutes of the first morning, this teacher and scholar of the Word gave us new tools of understanding through his use of a well-known parable. He reminded us that people *want* to know about faith, but it had to be true, life-changing, based on love, and meet them where they were! There was something more. In addition to his main points, Dr. Palmer gave us a golden nugget about faith. He said, "Over time, the gospel, which is the good news that Jesus loves us and died for us, *will* vindicate itself."

Of all the quotable remarks, this one stood out and caused me to reflect upon my life during the past twenty years! There I sat in the very town where, in 1976, the course of my life had abruptly changed like a weather vane unexpectedly being blown from north to south by the gust of a huge, strong wind. Once I had lived near this hotel as a completely addicted, emotionally wounded, and self-destructive young woman. At that time, my lifestyle and appearance would have been comparable to those of a morally loose, rowdy, lewd-mouthed, beer-drinking, bar-hopping twenty-one-year-old. (You can imagine how interesting it is to even search for the words that described me back then.) For the very reason that I was now sitting in a spiritual growth seminar rather than in a bar, it was obvious that anyone who knew me then would have to admit that I was a *completely different and much better* person than I had been in 1976.

I pondered the thought, *Had the gospel, over time, been vindicated in and through me?* Yes, beyond my wildest expectations.

At forty, I was healthier and more fit than I had been at sixteen *or* twenty-one! I had been sober for eighteen years, which had allowed my true personality, unbridled spirituality, and athletic ability to mature into an inspirational author, motivational speaker, and aerobics instructor. Without drink, but with God in me, I was still funny, much happier, and more excited about my life today than I was as a twenty-one-year-old drug addict and alcoholic!

I hadn't turned into a freak or a failure or a frump. I hadn't weirded out, as some people warned. Instead, faith had completed me, bestowing purpose and meaning into my life. I had become a successful author of ten books, owned my own company for the past ten years, had been faithfully married to one man for eighteen years, and was the mother of one great high school son. Yes, faith's influence *had a wonderful effect on my life over time!*

At the close of Dr. Palmer's talk, I asked Steve, a friend and former coworker of mine who had driven to the seminar, if he would mind giving me a ride to my aunt and uncle's house in Pebble Beach (about ten miles away) during the afternoon break. Prompted by the morning's lecture, I mentioned that *if there was time,* I would also like to see the places where my faith had become so real to me twenty years earlier. Though I had been back to Monterey a few times, I had never revisited those places.

At about 2:00 P.M., Steve and I drove out of the hotel parking lot. I was surprised that we were directly across from Tenth Avenue, which was only seconds away from my former house on Sixth Avenue. So, we headed straight to Sixth Avenue, and at the corner, I hopped out of the car and took a picture of the last place I had lived as an alcoholic and drug addict. At the sight of the little, odd, dilapidated pale yellow house, I shivered while I was bombarded with memories of wild parties, cat flea infestation, and my drug-addicted neighbors. It was eerie.

Then I recalled that only three blocks away was the home of the first Christian family I had ever met! At the time, *I even* thought they were odd because they would hold hands or, worse, raise their hands when they prayed! We drove the three short blocks, and again I jumped out of the car. From the middle of the street, I took a photo of the neatly groomed yard and country blue house. This time I smiled.

Next, we drove down to Highway 1, made a left, then veered right onto Cannery Row, planning to wind through Pacific Grove and enter Pebble Beach at the Asilomar entrance. My relatives were expecting me to arrive around 3:00 P.M. As we entered Cannery Row, again, a number of vivid memories flooded my mind—places where I had frequently gone drinking and dancing, the bay where I had gone kayaking in the moonlight, and the wharf restaurant where I had eaten squid and drank Jim Beam for the first time on my twenty-first birthday! Motivated by the thought of capturing another memory, but with little warning to Steve, I opened the car door and jumped out to take a picture of Monterey Bay. Steve hadn't anticipated this impulsive move, so he just made a U-turn and came back for me. Snapping only one picture, I returned to the car. Slowly, we started driving through the commercial section of the Cannery, looking at each storefront.

As if on cue, a fellow ran out of a store, motioning to a meter maid *not* to ticket his illegally parked truck. Apparently, he had been on the phone, but could see that she was going to give him a ticket if he didn't immediately move his vehicle. It became obvious that his truck was the vehicle we were just coming alongside of.

The person running out of the door didn't notice me, but I immediately realized that he was my old boyfriend, whom I had lived with for two years prior to becoming a

Christian. I hadn't seen or spoken to him in eighteen years. Steve was driving slowly enough that I asked him to stop, park, or pull over—and I got out of the car again.

Can you imagine this scene? As my old boyfriend, Kevin, ran across the street I called out, "Hello! Excuse me." No response, just a glance. Then I said, "Don't you recognize me?"

He turned, as if he recognized only the sound of my voice. Standing still and stunned in the middle of the street, he inquired, "Beck?"

With that acknowledgment, we walked over to his truck and seemed to pick up where we had left off—but not finished—twenty years earlier. He said, "What are you doing here?"

How ironic, I thought. *I'm at a seminar on* how to share my faith—*which is exactly what drove us apart twenty years ago—and I have to tell him . . . again!* I replied, "Do you really want to know?"

"Yeah," he said with a laugh. He seemed to want to know.

"Well, this is my friend Steve," I said, pointing to Steve who was walking up to join us. "We're attending the Billy Graham School of Evangelism at the Hyatt in Monterey. I just had lunch with my old boss (whom he knew) and we're on our way to see my aunt and uncle (whom he had met)," I added.

"Wow!" he said. It was probably the one word that described what we were all thinking. What were the odds of this chance encounter? This seemed too bizarre. Then as if I had a neon sign in my head, I began to think in terms of the words I had heard earlier that day: "Over time, the gospel will vindicate itself."

Was it just an incredible coincidence that we would meet *on that street on that day*? Or was it meant to be? What seemed most significant to me was not that I had lost Kevin more than twenty years ago, but that the relationship I had begun with Jesus back then in Monterey had not faded one iota. In fact, it had not been a fad or a crutch or a weird religion. In 1976, I had begun a personal relationship with God that had only grown stronger, more articulate, and deeper within me over time.

During the twenty minutes of our heart-to-heart conversation, most unexpectedly, much of the hidden pain and past shame that had been lodged deep within my heart for years felt as if it was evaporating, as we apologized for any hurt we might have caused the other.

Naturally, our discussion culminated in talking about my faith, my alcoholism, our shared past, and our current lives. Kevin agreed that where he stood with God hadn't changed, but he could see that faith had had a very good effect upon my life!

In the car was a condensed version of a book I had written in 1990, *Let Prayer Change Your Life*. I was planning to give it to my aunt and uncle. Instead, I offered it to Kevin! I thought he *just might* want to read about what happened to me twenty years ago, how much I've changed, and why. He did!

Unbelievably, after twenty years, but in the same setting, we parted with the same differences.

Did faith in God revolutionize my life? Yes. Was it appealing to others? Not at first. Not for a long time, to some. But *over time,* faith *proves* that it is relevant, meeting you right where you are at; it is relational, reminding you that it is based on a relationship with a living, loving God; it is radical because it is rooted in truth; and it is revolutionary because it brings change into your life that has a good effect!

Faith that is revolutionary results in significant changes *that are not* instigated by our will or thought processes, but initiated by the Holy Spirit of God who comes to live within us at the time we enter into a relationship with God. True faith *should, will,* and *does* transform our lives. The Bible puts it this way: "Therefore, if anyone is in Christ, he is a new creation; the old has gone, the new has come!" (2 Cor. 5:17).

■ ■ ■

True faith *should, will,* and *does* transform our lives.

■ ■ ■

What are the signs that a life has been revolutionized by God?

- SUPERNATURAL POWER is released!
- ENDURANCE is received!
- OBEDIENCE is an option!

- MIRACLES are bestowed!
- FORGIVENESS is given!
- LOVE is the mark!

SUPERNATURAL POWER IS RELEASED!

Throughout *Let Faith Change Your Life,* I have told a number of true-life stories that are extraordinary, dramatic, and convincing. In each case, the people involved experienced a powerful transformation that changed their lives forever. I believe that it was God's Holy Spirit who entered each one of them and filled them with His power *so that they could overcome their weaknesses.*

I want to share another first-person story that shows the supernatural, transforming power of God that is released when faith enters a person's life.

KAREN'S STORY

My eyes struggled to focus as I began to awake. My heart and lungs were pounding, and everything seemed out of focus. I was drowning. Panic swept over me, and I began thrashing about, gasping for air. My head made a hollow thump as it hit the marble floor. Shaking violently, I managed to pull myself up off the floor. I was in the bathroom of my Manhattan apartment. I had been drinking heavily that night and must have blacked out. With sudden horror I realized that I had passed out in a bath I must have drawn earlier in the evening. When I was finally able to raise my eyes to meet my image in the mirror, I noticed my lips were blue, and the blood vessels underneath my eyes had broken. The shame I saw in my face was unbearable. *I was twenty-six years old. I wanted to die.*

When I look back at what my life was like then, I see two totally different people. These people were so different that one would not have associated with the other, except for the fact that both people existed inside me. The person the outside world saw was a successful career woman engaged to be married to a handsome attorney. I led a glamorous life. I was invited to all of the right parties, I vacationed in exciting, faraway places, and I had all the trappings of success. Despite all of my worldly success, on the inside I was incredibly unhappy. I felt that there was an enormous void in my life. Nothing I had ever accomplished could make me like the person I was. I had tried to fill the emptiness I always felt with a myriad of material belongings. When those things did not work, I was left feeling resentful and angry. I focused the anger inward, and it quickly turned to self-hatred. I sought escape from the feelings and found it in alcohol. I am not sure when I crossed the line from social drinking to alcoholism, but it did not take long.

However, the friend I found in drinking soon betrayed me. As I drank more heavily, the periods of time that I could not remember, aka blackouts, grew more frequent. During those times, I had no idea who I had spoken to, where I had been, or what I had been doing. I was riddled with anxiety attacks during which my heart would race and my hands would shake uncontrollably. People were starting to suspect that something was wrong, but no one suspected that I—a young college-educated woman—could have a drinking problem! I became more determined than ever to keep up the double life I had been living. The months that ensued were the darkest of my life. Alcoholism had rendered me morally, emotionally, and spiritually bankrupt. It left me standing in my bathroom, staring at my reflection and contemplating suicide.

As I stood there, I remembered something my mother had said to me earlier that year: "How far down do you have to go before you will look up and ask the Lord to help you?" I fell to my knees and began praying for help. I prayed desperately for guidance and forgiveness. My walk with the Lord began at that moment.

Shortly thereafter, I found myself watching the Billy Graham Crusade on television, and I recognized the face of Becky Tirabassi. Becky and I had grown up in the same town, and her faith had always been an inspiration to me. I knew the Lord was guiding me, and I quickly tracked her telephone number down and actually located her in a hotel while she was at one of her speaking engagements. Becky and I hadn't spoken in years, and I wasn't sure if I could find the courage to share with her what a mess I had made of my life. I thought back to the time she had been my Campus Life director in high school, and I knew she would not judge me. When we spoke, I openly and honestly shared my feelings of

despair with her as well as the problems I was having with
alcohol. We prayed for me to open my heart to the love of
Jesus Christ, to accept Him into my life as my personal
Savior.

My rebirth into the light of Christ's love has been a daily
journey. I pray each morning and night for His will to be
done in my life. I trust in Jesus with all of my heart, and I
know that He is always with me. Today I am at peace with
myself, and my desire to drink alcohol has been completely
lifted. I have been relieved of worrying about the future and
regretting the past because I know I will never be any more
or less than what the Lord has planned for me. I am so grateful to the Lord for each day that I have to live and the opportunity that I have to share His love with others.

In a few weeks, I begin classes to become an alcoholism
counselor with the hope that I can help others who suffer
from addiction. I believe that the Lord has a plan for my life,
and it will be revealed throughout my walk with Him. I am
encouraged by Isaiah 41:10, which says, "Do not fear, for I
am with you; do not be dismayed, for I am your God. I will
strengthen you and help you; I will uphold you with my
righteous right hand."

This is not an isolated incident. You need only change
the type of addiction or problem, the place, or the era, and
you will be able to tell another person's equally dramatic
story or testimony of how God's supernatural power revolutionized a life!

When people exhibit *new* power to overcome an *old* weakness, I contend that this *is evidence* that the living God lives within them. These changes become powerful proof to all those who witness them that what people could not do on their own *is possible* with God's power—His Holy Spirit—within them! Instead of being under the influence of drugs, alcohol, money, or power, people who ask God to come into and change their lives will experience the supernatural power of the Holy Spirit of God released in them!

In *The Holy Spirit,* Billy Graham explains that "God the Holy Spirit gives us power for a purpose—power to help us glorify God in every dimension of our lives. In the Christian life, power is dynamically related to a Person. This Person is the Holy Spirit Himself, indwelling the Christian and filling him with the fullness of His power."

If the Holy Spirit's function is to give glory to God, a transformed life is a visual sign or confirmation that Someone powerful—yet unseen—has become a real, indwelling part of us!

ENDURANCE IS RECEIVED!

My friends, Todd and Anna Marie, recently found a tumor the size of a small potato on the back of their very petite four-year-old daughter, Sarah. The discovery of this tumor created many serious concerns. Was it cancer? Was it a genetic disorder? How soon would it have to come out? Was the tumor attached to the spinal cord? Would there be a great deal of pain involved?

The doctor who would be operating on Sarah had recently relocated to a large children's hospital in Orange County, California, very close to my house. Todd, Anna Marie, and Sarah flew in from Idaho a few days before the operation. Because I lived so close, I planned to visit Sarah in the hospital sometime during their stay.

I called and spoke to Anna Marie on the night of the operation. She was very calm. We talked and prayed for quite a while, discussing the inevitable difficulties of recovery as well as the uncertainty of the diagnosis that was still ahead. The operation had gone longer and appeared more serious than they had first anticipated. More muscle had to be removed than previously thought, and little Sarah had quite a large incision, which they did not want to fill with fluid if she was to heal quickly.

I called Anna Marie on the following day to say that I would be stopping in briefly around 5:00 P.M. Parking at hospitals is always a trial. Only when I got there did I realize that I had no money with me for the garage attendant! My eyes scanned the streets for a free spot—just as the little car ahead of me appeared to get the last one . . . no, there was one more on the corner! I slipped right into the end spot and ran one block to the entrance, past the counter without getting a pass, and inadvertently took the long way to Room 318. Having been in a hurry, I was also embarrassed that I hadn't brought a little gift for Sarah.

When I entered the room, I saw a tiny child with beautiful long, wavy, dark brown hair lying on her stomach. Her arm was hooked up to needles and machines, enough to make me a bit woozy.

Unsure of where and how to begin talking with a little child who was so ill, I noticed the coloring books by her bed. In fact, I noticed *everything* by her bed. All of the little books and toys and music had something to do with God. I briefly reflected on that: If I was the mother of a child in this situation, where would I find my strength? How could I be an encouragement to my child? It was my quick conclusion that I, too, would have relied on God as our constant companion throughout the entire ordeal.

It was obvious that Anna Marie and Sarah shared a comfortable three-way relationship with each other and God. Since birth, little Sarah had gone to church, sung Bible songs, read Bible stories, and as a toddler, she had chosen to believe in the God of the Bible as her own heavenly Father. Now, they held on tightly to their faith in their God to give them endurance for this fight.

Quietly, Sarah asked her mommy if she and I could color in her new coloring book. Because she couldn't move her hand or back muscles, I offered to color Joseph's coat of many colors with the crayons that Sarah assigned to me! It was a sweet, enjoyable time. We prayed together and I left.

The next day, there was not much new news, but Sarah had a lot of pain to deal with. At the last minute, I decided to go to the hospital again, though the visiting hours had already ended. As I headed onto the empty freeway toward the hospital, I was reminded of the many moments I had spent in prayer for Sarah, her parents, and the doctor over the past week.

I wondered what an illness would be like if you didn't have faith in God. What would sustain you if you didn't believe that He heard your every prayer, sigh, or groan? How could you find words to express yourself if you didn't have the comforting words of the Bible to ease and guide and lead you toward God at a time like this? How *could* a mother handle her child's pain if she didn't know and believe that her heavenly Father loved her child more than she did?

When I sneaked up to the room this time, I found a small group had collected . . . a cousin, a grandmother, a grandfather, a father, and a mother, who was softly playing a guitar, quietly singing praise songs to the Lord at the foot of the bed of their little loved one. I entered the room to the smiles of those who knew that I shared their faith. In fact, my unexpected appearance seemed to strengthen them.

I joined in the singing, but kept my eyes focused on little Sarah. I kept thinking, *Is there something more that I can do?* I could see how faith was the greatest resource this family had—giving them endurance to face every bit of news, every bout with pain, every emotional pang. I asked, "Has anyone laid hands on Sarah and anointed her with oil?" No, no one had—as of yet. We all agreed that it would be a wonderful idea, but not a nurse or a purse could produce any type of oil! I had not come prepared, but as a last resort, I used a little leftover salad dressing and touched it gently to Sarah's forehead. Our little group of believers laid hands upon her tiny body and held each other's hands as we prayed as the Bible directs those who pray for the sick. We were encouraged with the peace that comes from knowing God.

Once Sarah returned home, the barrage of test results began to filter in. Sarah's problem was traced to a genetic disease, so Todd, Sarah's father, was tested as well.

Within one week, Todd himself was diagnosed with a form of cancer and the same genetic disease as his daughter. He underwent a serious surgery and now faces the unknown, but not alone.

The Callaghan family has received more devastating news in one year than any other family I have personally known. When X rays and MRIs were a daily requirement, or when the waiting seemed unbearable or the doctors expressed helplessness, the Callaghans had only one place to find the endurance necessary to face another needle, surgery, or test. Endurance was received when they placed their faith in God.

Recently, I left a message on their answering machine, just letting them know that I was praying for them and thinking about them! I had remembered Anna Marie telling me that a next possible step would be a trip to the Cleveland Clinic in Ohio.

On Tuesday afternoon, I got a return call from Anna Marie with an update. She told me that she, Sarah, and Todd were leaving for Cleveland in the morning and would be there until Friday.

Knowing how her faith must have been waning through the emotionally and physically draining weeks and months, I mentioned my former church as a possible oasis for her while they were in Cleveland. I gave her the phone number of the church and my former pastor's name, Tom (who had just officiated at my father's homecoming service), and I mentioned that this church had a Wednesday night service. I even told her that I thought on some Wednesday nights, they prayed for the sick. Last of all, I gave her the phone number of my mother, whom she had never met, but who lived in Cleveland. She knew that both of them were a part of a group of people who daily prayed for me.

My mother called me on Friday night and said, "Guess who I just saw?"

I asked, "Who?"

She said, "Anna Marie called me. She called our church on Wednesday when they got into Cleveland and talked with Pastor Tom, and he invited her to the Wednesday night service. Anna Marie, Todd, and Sarah were asked to share their story with the whole congregation. When they were finished telling how faith in God has gotten them through each day, many in the congregation laid hands on them and prayed for them! They all felt as if the Callaghans had gone to church there for years!"

My mom had uncharacteristically worked late that Wednesday, so she did not go to the midweek service. But on Friday evening, Anna Marie and my mom met for the first time at the Callaghans' departure gate at the Cleveland airport. Though perfect strangers before that moment, they talked and prayed, encouraging and comforting each other.

There is no promise that faith is free of suffering, but within each day we can receive resources and power for endurance that come from prayer, singing praises, the laying on of hands, and the comfort and presence of the Holy Spirit.

Philip Yancey is a well-known author of numerous books on understanding pain and suffering and their relationship to God. In *Where Is God When It Hurts?* he writes,

> As I visited those whose pain far exceeded my own, I was surprised by its effects. Suffering was as likely to produce strengthened faith as to sow agnosticism. My anger about pain has melted mostly for one reason: I have come to know God. He has given me joy and love and happiness and goodness. They have come in flashes, in the midst of my confused, unrighteous world, but their presence has been absolute enough to convince me that my God is worthy of trust. Knowing Him is worth all the enduring.

"Where does that leave me when I stand next to a hospital bed?" he asks. "It leaves me with a solid faith in a Person which no amount of suffering can erode."

"Where is God when it hurts?" he asks. "He has promised supernatural strength to nourish our spirit, even if our physical suffering goes unrelieved."

141

Only a relevant, relational faith in the God of the Bible brings strangers together in a strange city and makes them "family." Only a revolutionary faith in the living, loving God gives people courage to hold on, to endure, and to keep on trusting in the midst of suffering! Without this faith, we would be sorely tempted to give in to hopelessness, depression, self-pity, and anguish. With faith, we can endure!

■ ■ ■

Only a revolutionary faith in the living, loving God gives people courage to hold on, to endure, and to keep on trusting in the midst of suffering!

■ ■ ■

OBEDIENCE IS AN OPTION!

It takes an awfully good reason to deny yourself something that you want *simply* because people have asked you to do it for them in their way. It takes a certain level of trust and respect to cancel out, change, or give up your plans and desires in order to give in or acquiesce.

The topic of "authority" can elicit a very volatile discussion in our current culture and society. To be subject to, submit to, sacrifice for, and obey are concepts that can stir up strong reaction, especially in people who have been abused, taken advantage of, or disappointed by those who have been in authority over them.

I recently heard a speaker mention that being under

someone's authority has never been a popular idea in the United States. He reminded us that monarchs and lords were thrown out of America hundreds of years ago. We're a country of strong, proud, and independent people. That is why it should be no surprise that some of us wrestle with the idea of submitting to God. It actually becomes a barrier to even considering, much less entering into, a relationship with Him. However, a revolutionary faith hinges on believing that God is relevant to the times, relational in His approach, radical because He can be tested and trusted, and revolutionary in His ability to bring change into our lives.

In the third chapter of the book of Daniel, there is a story of three young men, Shadrach, Meshach, and Abednego, who were followers of the God of Abraham, Isaac, and Jacob. Unfortunately, their entire lives were disrupted when they were exiled to a foreign country that did not worship or respect their God. After a time, they were told to stop worshiping their God and informed they must worship King Nebuchadnezzar *or else* they would be thrown into a fiery furnace. Herein lies their defining moment. History records that because their loyalty to and trust in God were so great, they refused to denounce Him, even though it might result in death.

Ultimately, their loyalty and obedience to God *were* costly. Just before the three Israelite men were cast into the furnace, Daniel 3:16–18 records their words to the king who was very angry with them: "O Nebuchadnezzar, we do not need to defend ourselves before you in this matter. If we are thrown into the blazing furnace, the God we serve is able to save us from it, and he will rescue us from your hand, O king. But even if he does not, we want you to know, O king, that we will not serve your gods or worship the image of gold you have set up."

The king was so furious that he threw these men, firmly tied up, into the flaming furnace. When the king looked into the fire to see their demise, he realized that they were no longer tied up, but walking around with what appeared to be a fourth, godlike figure. He ordered them to be removed from the furnace and found not a hair on their heads was singed, their robes were not scorched, and they did not smell of fire.

The king had encountered men with a revolutionary faith that stood strong in the face of temptation. They could have saved their own lives by denying God, but instead they chose to be obedient and loyal to Him. The result? The king said,

> *Praise be to the God of Shadrach, Meshach and Abednego, who has sent his angel and rescued his servants! They trusted in him and defied the king's command and were willing to give up their lives rather than serve or worship any god except their own God. Therefore I decree that the people of any nation or language who say anything against the God of Shadrach, Meshach and Abednego be cut into pieces and their houses be turned into piles of rubble, for no other god can save in this way* (Dan. 3:28–29).

Only people with a revolutionary faith will believe, follow, and obey a God that they cannot see. But you can be certain that this depth of loyalty has not come from demand. It could only be a response of love. People do not willingly obey and follow a tyrant who demands unrealistically of them. Obviously, these men had been in a relationship with God prior to their furnace experience, and they had found Him worthy of their devotion.

In our lifetimes, very few of us will be asked to obey God to the point of physical death. We might, though, be asked to follow Him to the point of humility or sacrifice. I believe that obedience to God—as a response of love—is a way of life for those of us who know God. I submit that people with a revolutionary faith are willing to make choices that *please God* above ourselves.

■ ■ ■

I believe that obedience to God—as a response of love—is a way of life for those of us who know Him.

■ ■ ■

BILL'S STORY

When my dad died in 1949, I was forced to drop out of college and work full time to help support my mother, who had never worked. With my extensive background in sports, having lettered in sports in high school and attended college on an athletic scholarship, sporting goods seemed a natural business opportunity. With $2,500, no credit, and little business sense, I began a sporting goods business in Parma, Ohio. I figured I could just do it.

Displays and merchandise arrived, the store was decorated, the doors opened, and to my surprise few customers came in because inventory was small and selection was limited. I believe that the people who did patronize the store came because I knew so many people in the community over the years, but it wasn't enough. Some days total sales were fifty cents or one dollar. About two weeks after I opened, I realized that unless something changed I was going to go out of business just about as quickly as I went into business.

I proceeded to get a night job working for Tinnerman Products Company in Cleveland, Ohio. I would go in to work at 4:30 in the afternoon and work until 1:00 A.M. Then I would open the sporting goods store the next morning at 8:30 and work until 4:00. My mother would close the store for me between 6:00 and 7:00 P.M.

During this period my wife, Ruth, had our first child, Karen. The money I was making at Tinnerman was just about enough to support myself and my family. Looking for more income, I went into construction. I would work from 7:30 A.M. until 4:30 P.M. and then hurry to the sporting goods store to keep it open until 10:00. I continued on this track for approximately three years—working dual jobs and struggling. Every dollar earned in the store was plowed back into inventory; I took no income out of the store.

Finally, after the third year we started to come into the

black a little bit. Profits improved, and from the fourth through the sixth year we developed a solid service reputation and people from neighboring communities came to the store. At the time I also wrote a column on hunting and fishing in the local paper.

However, the discount houses opened at the same time and immediately took the cream right off of the top from us. Many people came into our store to investigate products and then purchased them at the discount houses. In an effort to diversify and avoid the discount price competition, we moved into the marine business in 1957–58. We were considered a successful retailer at the time—even winning the Annual Retailer Award for the United States—but I knew differently. We kept pouring every dollar back into inventory, and I was still struggling to meet the payables, payroll, taxes, and other obligations of business ownership. It got to the point where I was eating, sleeping, and breathing this business.

I found that I paid a high price for this fast-track lifestyle. My wife became both mother and father to our children. As much as I loved them, I struggled in trying not to quit the business and in trying to build the business. I knew that I could cut corners on service or product quality to keep pace with the discount houses, but I couldn't bring myself to make an extra dollar at my customers' expense. As things grew more desperate, I had to decide between quitting or working longer, harder hours. I had thirteen years invested in this business, and I couldn't bring myself to quit. Yet money was so tight. I could see my competitors opening up on

Sundays, and I knew they were selling some boat motors without tuning them up and cutting other corners to make an extra dollar. But I just couldn't do these things.

I had always gone to church and always had prayer before our sales meetings. Like so many others, I was raised by the "be a good boy, have a good conscience, and do good things" philosophy. As I said, the discount businesses were opening up on Sundays, and while I didn't really want to open up on Sundays, I felt I had no choice if I was to meet the debt obligations of the business. Consequently, I went to church one Palm Sunday and opened up the store after returning from church—against the wishes of my family. Closing up after three or four hours on that Sunday afternoon, I felt unclean, and I wished I hadn't done it. The following Sunday I went to church and sang the first service with the choir. During the second sermon I was reflecting and meditating on part of my life and knew that many people would look at me and say I didn't have very good credit, that I was slow in paying bills.

No one, from my mother and Ruth to my accountant, could tell me to give up the business. They couldn't say, "Bill, throw in the towel." So I sat there in that choir loft thinking, *God, You know my heart. Humble me and just make me with You at this point.* Suddenly, Psalm 27:1 came to me, even though I didn't read the Bible at that time and didn't have it in memory: "The LORD is my light and my salvation; whom shall I fear? the LORD is the strength of my life; of whom shall I be afraid?" (KJV).

Right then and there I went out of a closely held

corporation and into a partnership with the Lord Jesus Christ. I would no longer trust in my wisdom and in my strength and my intellect, but I would turn it all over to Jesus. I didn't hear any bells or whistles or things ringing like some people have in the conversion experience. But I knew that I had changed and that my life had started to change. I gave up the sporting goods/marine business. It wasn't easy. There were thirteen years and $84,000 in paper lost. Yet I found peace, a peace that God promises in His Word, "the peace . . . which passeth all understanding" (Phil. 4:7 KJV).

From the time I prayed that small, yet powerful prayer, I experienced an immediate and insatiable urge to read the Bible. My wife noticed this new spiritual hunger in me, and she bought me my first study Bible. God miraculously put people in my path who were Christians, and I appreciated how they shared their faith with me and helped me grow.

One might expect that my business miraculously improved. In fact, it grew worse. Within the course of that following year (1963), I went to the bank to try to work out a reasonable plan for liquidating my business, one that would allow the family to remain employed at the shop while I pursued a new occupation in an attempt to regain financial stability. I was both shocked and disappointed when the bank would not renew my financing. I was forced to liquidate my store for pennies on the dollar. I lost everything and had to close the store, but I found more, much more—a personal relationship with Jesus Christ as Savior and Partner. At that time I made a personal vow to God: if I ever rebounded financially, I would pay back the $32,000 that shareholders had invested in my business.

Fortunately, by 1970 my venture into the insurance business had become very successful, and over a five-year period, I was able to completely pay back the investors from my failed business. With each of my regular payments, I included a letter, book, or pamphlet that named Christ as the reason for my ethical and professional behavior. The people were both surprised and grateful because I was no longer legally required to repay them! But I considered the repayment a personal and a spiritual matter; not only were my name and reputation at stake, but so were God's, my partner.

For more than thirty years, I have owned and managed a very successful insurance firm in northeastern Ohio. However, God, my wife of more than forty years, and my family have always remained the greatest priorities in my life.

I found strength in the Lord, and I found refuge just by receiving, believing, and trusting in Him. I have given Him all my talents and all my abilities to use as He will. I praise Him by humbling myself, and whatever talents I might have I try to use for Him because He must increase and I must decrease.

When you have a personal relationship with the living, loving God, obedience to Him is not a duty; it is a response of love. You understand that the God who loves you would only ask you to do what is right, just, loyal, loving, or possible for you to do. *Obedience to God is an option that both hurts and feels good!* A revolutionary faith obeys God instead of following one's own desires. It takes courage; it reaps personal reward, self-respect, and respect from others; and it gives you the knowledge that you have pleased your Father in heaven.

■ ■ ■

Obedience to God is an option that both hurts and feels good!

■ ■ ■

MIRACLES ARE BESTOWED!

Last year, a friend's mother was diagnosed with a very serious cancer that needed an immediate operation. Over coffee the day before her mom's operation, I shared with my friend the biblical principles from James 5 of "laying on of hands" and "anointing the sick with oil." Because these are biblical principles, we discussed them as powerful resources *meant* to be used by all believers. I suggested that she and her family might have a time of "laying on of hands" with her mother.

Within a few hours, my friend called me back to ask if my husband and I could meet them at the hospital. She had gathered her relatives (who were believers) to congregate at her mother's room at four that afternoon to pray! We gladly agreed!

Just before leaving the house, I reread the verses in James 5 in order to better prepare myself for our time together. I was struck by something new. Verse 16 says, "Confess your sins to each other . . . so that you may be healed. The prayer of a righteous man is powerful and effective." We had planned to bring oil and lay our hands on her mother, but this section on confession gave me a new idea.

When we entered the hospital room, a small group of about eight people had gathered. My friend asked if *I* would like to lead us in the healing prayers! I wasn't an expert at this, so I started out by reading aloud the four verses in James 5. At the conclusion, I said, "Because these words direct those who are praying for the sick to confess *their* sins, I feel that we should each take a moment to do that *before* we lay hands on your mom and anoint her with oil. Let's break up into twos—with someone you are comfortable with—and confess anything in your life that might hinder you from being a powerful and effective pray-er at this time!"

At first there was a bit of hesitation. Then each caught the eye of one other person, and every pair found a quiet corner of the room or section of the hallway in which to make verbal confessions of any unresolved anger or bitterness or so forth in our lives that could hinder us from praying effective healing prayers. Because I was not a family member, I offered to receive and give "confession" with my friend's mother. It was an unusual spiritual experience, but each person sensed that the biblical purpose behind this concept was powerful. After we confidentially shared with each other, we prayed to God in our pairs, asking for forgiveness for any of our specific sins. We quietly regrouped and laid hands on my friend's mother, anointing her with oil.

We would not know the outcome of the chemotherapy or surgery for months, yet by following the principle for healing prayers as prescribed in the Bible, we gained peace and confidence that we had taken a deliberate action step in asking God for healing in her mother's life.

I can now report that her mother has been in remission for more than a year and is doing very well! In addition, she recently told me that most people have a lot of nausea with this particular chemotherapy, yet she did not experience any!

No one can force God to do anything, much less bestow a miracle. But I believe that there are three steps that we can take if we want to be prepared or in position for God to do a miracle in our lives.

James 5:16 says, "Confess your sins to each other . . . so that you may be healed." In addition, Psalm 84:11 says, "No good thing does [God] withhold from those whose walk is blameless." First, search your heart and mind for anything in your life that needs to be changed, turned from, left behind, confessed, forgiven, or resolved. After you have done that, without delay do whatever you need to do to right the wrongs or make amends.

I am convinced that taking a personal inventory—and making amends or corrections—is a rudimentary step for those who are praying to receive a healing or a miracle. But I do not consider this step necessarily defamatory. I *never assume* that illness is a result of sin, but I do believe that a healing or a miracle is a much greater possibility for those who have confessed any known shortcomings in their lives.

This first step is not just a good idea, but a stated biblical principle.

Second, essential to obtaining a miracle or a healing is the admission that God is powerful enough to change your circumstances. If your confidence in God is limited or finite, then your faith in what He can do will be limited as well. The object of your faith cannot be your passion for healing, the visible circumstances of a situation, or your past history—good or bad. It is the present condition of being in a right relationship with God and acknowledging that He is all-powerful in any situation. A sure faith is able to ask the *God who is able* to do that which is otherwise impossible.

We cannot muster up faith or try harder or believe more in order to experience a miracle or a healing. But we can increase in faith by reading God's Word. Romans 10:17 says, "Consequently, faith comes from hearing the message, and the message is heard through the word of Christ." By reading the Bible, we learn more about God and how He has worked, giving us confidence and patterns to show us how He will work.

Faith understands that God *is able* to heal, intervene, and help. It acknowledges that the God of the Bible is powerful enough to do the impossible. A sound faith has seen and knows that not always, but often, God bestows a miracle of healing.

Finally, the third step to experiencing a miracle is simply and specifically *asking* God to do it. Asking is not negotiating with Him, arm wrestling, debating, or demanding of Him.

Asking is an attitude of humility, dependency, and worship that is present in the one who wants God to do what no person or machine or nation can do. Faith is accepting His authority and sovereignty and power and strength and omniscience—as well as His answer.

A strong faith acknowledges that God can, is able, and is powerful enough to do a miracle. A revolutionary faith can ask God to do the impossible and wait with expectation for His answer.

FORGIVENESS IS GIVEN!

The practice of forgiveness is fundamental to possessing a revolutionary faith. Be assured, it isn't the expected reaction to an offense, nor does forgiveness come naturally when you've been wounded. Yet the power of forgiveness has the ability to turn an entire nation, city, company, family, or relationship around. Only pride or pain, personality or position, can hinder a person from forgiving.

In *God's Little Devotional Book,* there is a story told about a young Korean exchange student who had been brutally murdered in 1958 by a gang of teenage boys. The parents and family of the victim did something highly unusual and most unprecedented. They not only sent a letter to those in charge of the punishment due the teenagers who murdered their son, but they also started a fund for the "religious, educational, vocational, and social guidance of the boys" upon their release. They wanted their letter and offer of funds to be received "with a spirit received from the gospel of our Lord Jesus Christ who died for our sins."

Put in that situation, who could react and respond with such compassion and absolute forgiveness? Only those with a revolutionary faith!

Forgiveness is undeniably and uniquely difficult to extend because it has the ability to be withheld. Often, it takes more than a big emotional breath before we will forgive. We might struggle through an agonizing search of self or feel physically nauseated at the thought of letting go of the resentment we hold toward an offender. But when forgiveness is given, the effects are immeasurable:

It can mend deep emotional scars in seconds.

It can stop tears.

It can elicit smiles and embraces.

It can force open shut doors.

It has the power to heal.

God Himself asks those who are in a relationship with Him to exercise forgiveness in our lives. And He gives us only one reason.

He forgave us . . .

- when we didn't deserve it,
- while we were yet separated from Him, and
- though we rejected His love.

There is no greater example of forgiveness than God's forgiveness toward us.

LOVE IS THE MARK!

It is no secret that the greatest commandments in the Bible are to love God with all your heart, soul, and body, and to love your neighbor as yourself.

If loving God—whom you can't see—isn't difficult enough, how is a naturally selfish person able to sacrificially love another person when (1) that person does not deserve it, (2) it isn't convenient, or (3) it would cost too much? Love is perhaps the most difficult aspect of faith to understand, but it is the most obvious indication that you possess it!

In *The God Who Is There,* Francis A. Schaeffer claims that the true "mark of faith" is love. Most people would agree that (1) faith *should* have a tangible, outward appearance and that (2) love would certainly be a noble attribute of faith. But Schaeffer expects more when he states that "the world should have the right to look upon believers and make a judgment about them based on their ability to love."

Let's assume that he is correct. Then we might also assume that there are a great number of observers in America who are wondering, *Just where are* these people of faith? If the faithful in America are those identified by a particular religion or religious group, then observers might question the infighting, backstabbing, and infidelity that overshadow their love for others.

Perhaps love is not the "mark of faith" that my generation or country has been corporately exhibiting or is currently known by. Perhaps only Mother Teresa and a few others have gained international recognition as those who have the "mark of faith." But I believe that there *are* great numbers of individuals in our local churches and synagogues who exhibit an extraordinary amount of love to their neighbors, community, and family every day.

Like my mom. She is one of the faithful ones who regularly deliver food and clothing to the hungry and homeless. At seventy-five years old, only days after her husband had died, she took her monthly shift at the Salvation Army to feed the hungry and give clothing to the poor. The following month, when not enough volunteers came to hand out food and clothes, she worked a double shift, day and night, in order to meet the needs of those who are hurting. She has done this for years—out of love.

Others who have a revolutionary love make it a habit to visit the imprisoned to share God's message of hope and forgiveness with them. They take Bibles, lead meetings, and even help in special ways to extend love to the prisoners' children.

There are those who, despite being busy themselves, volunteer to help the sick and elderly, considering them to be a part of the extended family of God. Then there are the ones who are never too busy to listen to a concern, pray for a sick family member, or financially assist when the need is shared. They remember the lonely, widowed, and orphaned with

Christmas gifts, birthday cards, thoughtful notes, and financial assistance.

There are the faithful who . . .

- invite you into their homes,
- include you in their activities, and
- speak up for you when you are not strong enough to speak for yourself.

They do not notice a person's color or income.

They do not wound with their words, or they are always quick to apologize.

They are not sacrificial with their love because people are watching them, or because it could win them a vote or make them more popular.

What could possibly inspire people to love in this way?

I believe that it is *God's love toward them* that motivates them to love others. Second Corinthians 1:3–4 gives us more insight into this: "Praise be to the God and Father of our Lord Jesus Christ, the Father of compassion and the God of all comfort, who comforts us in all our troubles, so that we can comfort those in any trouble with the comfort we ourselves have received from God."

A revolutionary faith . . .

- loves when love is not expected.
- doesn't expose another's failure to make matters worse.
- doesn't take revenge.
- doesn't turn its back on another's suffering or plight.

It responds. It gives sacrificially.

It doesn't hate, ignore, abuse, or destroy another for any reason.

A person with this love will stand out as unusual in a world that hates, withholds, rejects, judges, hoards, and wounds.

■ ■ ■

A revolutionary faith . . . loves when love is not expected.

■ ■ ■

If you've met people with a revolutionary faith, they have left a mark on your life. And if you've asked them why or how they can love extraordinarily, unconditionally, and abundantly, they will tell you because . . .

God loved them when they didn't deserve it.

God forgave them when they hadn't earned it.

God paid a price for them that they could never pay.

God sent His Son to show them how much He loved them.

God did it all for love, not to manipulate or control.

If you have met people or attended a church with a revolutionary faith, then you have met people who are able to love—not because they are terrific, kind people but because they acknowledge that God first loved them.

14

A

REVOLUTIONARY

FAITH . . .

REQUIRES A RESPONSE

LAST WINTER I stayed in the hotel adjacent to the CNN Center while in Atlanta for a training event. During a break, Carissa (my assistant) and I walked into the Media Store at the CNN Center—just to browse. Each corner of the store had an interesting gimmick to it, but the area we gravitated toward was a mock television news set with a live camera, cameraman, and microphone. For a small fee, anyone could be videotaped as a newscaster reading that day's news with the aid of a TelePrompTer. Carissa knows me well enough to know that I might have a little fun with the whole idea, so having found that corner of the store before me, she called me over and egged me on until I consented to the taping.

As I gave the script an initial run-through, I have to admit that I was trying to impress the fellow behind the camera who seemed a little surprised at how comfortable I was in front of the camera. After he dubbed a lead-in by Larry King that introduced me as the "guest newscaster," my personal cameraman filmed the short "taping" in one take!

As Carissa and I walked up to the counter to pay for the tape, two other salesmen and the cameraman engaged us in a spirited conversation.

The youngest fellow said, "I bet that was the best thing you did today!"

I thought about it, then replied, "Actually, no."

He inquired, "What could have been better?"

"Well," I started slowly as I realized three pairs of eyes were intently upon me, "I gave a motivational talk for three hours today in front of an audience!"

A few flippant remarks followed . . . "Oh, so that's why you're so comfortable in front of a camera?"

Carissa came alive at this point. She said, "Actually, Becky has made a few videos of her own and has been in front of a camera quite a few times. She's an inspirational author, speaker, and fitness instructor."

One of the other clerks chimed in, "Inspirational? We can use a little inspiration right now!"

I joked, "What's wrong? A little morale problem?" They looked at each other and laughed.

Then the cameraman returned to the previous topic and asked, "What type of inspirational talk did you give today?"

All three young men had moved to the edge of the

counter to get closer to us. The third young man asked, "Yeah . . . what exactly did you speak about?"

"I talk about faith," I said, wondering if I would see blank stares or embarrassed glances or receive disinterested disclaimers from these young men.

"Oh, we could use some of that," they all chimed in—to my surprise!

The cameraman continued to look directly into my eyes and asked, "Faith? What do you say about faith?"

"I have almost finished writing a book called *Let Faith Change Your Life.*" With this captive audience of three young men in their twenties focused in rapt attention, I began to articulate my convictions.

"I talk about a faith that is relevant to all people, meeting them right where they're at! I discuss the many misconceptions about faith, sharing that I believe that faith is based on having a relationship with a living, loving God *and not a religion.*"

Before I could continue, the cameraman asked, "Faith in God? Which God?"

His Middle East skin color and direct question gave me the impression that he was well aware that the word *God* did not have the same meaning to every person. So I answered, "I talk about faith in the God *of the Bible.*"

"Oh, okay," he replied, very accepting, somewhat curious, but obviously not offended.

I was completely surprised by how each of them appeared to be hungry for more of my short "inspirational" presentation. I continued without hesitation, noticing the line of people wanting to purchase items was getting longer. (The three young men had temporarily forgotten that no one was manning the cash register.)

"The faith that I speak of is also radical, rooted in truth that is based on fact, recorded in history and time." I was ready to further articulate those points, but the three young men seemed to sense the depth of my convictions and were simply poised for more.

"The last thing that I believe about faith is that it is revolutionary—that it brings *change* into your life and has a good effect." As if on cue, the three young men pulled out their business cards and asked if I would send them a copy of my book! I hadn't even told them *how much* God had changed my life or *how wonderful* those changes had been!

Telling people about God is not something you *do*. It is an enthusiastic expression of who you know!

People who are unashamedly compelled to tell others about their faith in the God of the Bible do not do it because they are good at it or have been asked to do it, but because . . .

- they have found faith to be relevant to every part of their being.
- they have known no other person who has been so forgiving and loving toward them as God Himself.
- they are convinced that God's "good news" is true.
- they have experienced faith's revolution in their lives.

And they *keep* telling others about the God of the Bible, even at the risk of being misunderstood, rejected, sworn at, or whispered about. Why?

When you've experienced the *love* of God, you are not ashamed of the gospel, but are compelled to tell others about the most powerful Person who has changed—even revolutionized—your life.

This is the very reason I have written this book. From the time that Christ entered my life, my greatest passion and desire has been to present faith in a manner that could be shared, enjoyed, experienced, and embraced by those who are truly looking for change in their lives. I know faith to be transforming. I know it to be powerful and life-changing. And I know no other topic that can create more tension and misunderstanding than faith.

Therefore, throughout this book, I have tried to show you a faith that is relevant *not just for some,* but for all. I believe that I have shared a variety of stories that prove that faith meets not just the lonely, the emotional, and the broken but also the successful, the intellectual, and the misinformed.

Yet so many of us in America continue to stumble over faith because we think that it is based on a rigid religious system, or that it is a noble idea, or that God is a vague, mystical "it." Through every page of this book, I have tried—and agonized over how—to reveal to you a faith that is *much more.* Why? Because I am absolutely convinced that this faith, if you welcome it into your life, will *change* your life.

That is why I have stated, over and over, that the

transforming power of faith hinges on a relationship with the living, loving God, who in time and history created the world and all that is in it, who continuously cares for all of His creation, and who communicates with us through His Word, His Son, and the world. I believe it is our relationship with God, not our knowledge of a higher power whom *some* call "God," that is crucial to owning and maintaining a vibrant, exciting faith.

Even as I write this, I know that there are those of you who have been hindered from considering faith because you thought it was risky. I would like to suggest that it is not risky, but radical in a culture where absolutes and truths are questioned, where right is somehow wrong, and wrong is somehow right. In a time and era when every moral standard is being stampeded or tossed aside, only a faith that believes that the Bible is true and that Jesus was God who came to earth in the flesh can stand!

I am equally confident that when—not *if*—the realities of life, such as death, illness, disappointment, failed businesses, or relationships, touch your life, you will desperately search inwardly and outwardly for enough hope, courage, strength, or even a miracle to effect a powerful change in your life. I propose that the faith I have spoken of is *alone* powerful enough to bring change into your life that has a good and lasting effect.

Here is the defining truth: Faith is someone else's unless it is personally possessed.

How will you know if you or others possess faith?

Faith is not invisible, yet indwells you.

Faith often requires you to believe what you cannot see.

Faith is a belief of the heart *and the mind* that the person of Jesus Christ lived and died for you, that He was resurrected and lives today. A person who possesses faith—young or old, educated or poor—acknowledges that each individual is a sinner who needs a Savior.

Faith is entering into a personal relationship with an unseen God. Faith completes you, infusing you with purpose for your life on earth and a promise for eternal life with God in heaven. It is supernatural. It is life-changing. It is not only a partnership with God, but also being part of the family of God. This faith brings great change into your life that has a good effect.

■   ■   ■

Faith is accepting the person of Jesus Christ as the Son of God who loves you, died for you, lives for you, and longs to live within you.

■   ■   ■

Faith requires a response.

It cannot be earned or bought, though faith is not free. Someone paid for it for you and me. Faith is accepting the person of Jesus Christ as the Son of God who loves you, died for you, lives for you, and longs to live within you. He does not force His way into your life. He meets you. He loves you. He makes promises that only He can keep. He is able to bring change into your life. He waits for you to invite Him into your life. He leaves the decision up to you.

BIBLIOGRAPHY

Blackaby, Henry, and Claude V. King. *Experiencing God*. Nashville, Tenn.: Broadman and Holman, 1994.

Colson, Charles W. *Born Again*. Old Tappan, N.J.: Chosen, 1976.

————. *Loving God*. Grand Rapids, Mich.: Zondervan, 1983.

Graham, Billy. *The Holy Spirit*. Waco: Word, 1978.

Griffin, William, and Ruth Graham Dienert, comps. *The Faithful Christian*. New York: McCracken Press, 1994.

Hallesby, O. *Prayer*. Minneapolis: Augsburg, 1931.

Job, Rueben P., and Norman Shawchuck. *A Guide to Prayer for Ministers and Other Servants*. Nashville, Tenn.: The Upper Room, 1983.

Larson, Bruce. *Ask Me to Dance*. Waco: Word, 1972.

Lewis, C. S. *Mere Christianity*. New York: Macmillan, 1943.

Lucado, Max. *God Came Near*. Sisters, Oreg.: Multnomah, 1987.

Manning, Brennan. *The Ragamuffin Gospel*. Sisters, Oreg.: Multnomah, 1990.

Mason, Mike. *The Gospel According to Job*. Wheaton, Ill.: Crossway, 1994.

McDowell, Josh. *Evidence That Demands a Verdict*. San Bernardino, Calif.: Here's Life Publishers, 1972.

————. *More Than a Carpenter*. Wheaton, Ill.: Tyndale, 1977.

McDowell, Josh, and Bill Wilson. *A Ready Defense*. San Bernardino, Calif.: Here's Life Publishers, 1990.

Moore, Thomas. *Care of the Soul*. New York: HarperCollins, 1994.

Packer, J. I. *Knowing God*. Downers Grove, Ill.: InterVarsity Press, 1973.

Pascal, Blaise. *Pascal Pensées*. Harmondsworth, England: Penguin, 1966.

Robinson, Haddon W. *Biblical Preaching*. Grand Rapids, Mich.: Baker Book House, 1980.

Schaeffer, Francis A. *The Complete Works of Francis A. Schaeffer: A Christian Worldview*. Vol. 1, *A Christian View of Philosophy and Culture*. Westchester, Ill.: Crossway, 1982.

> *The God Who Is There*
>
> *Escape from Reason*
>
> *He Is There and He Is Not Silent*
>
> *Back to Freedom and Dignity*

———. *The Complete Works of Francis A. Schaeffer: A Christian Worldview*. Vol. 2, *A Christian View of the Bible as Truth*. Westchester, Ill.: Crossway, 1982.

> *Genesis in Space and Time*
>
> *No Final Conflict*
>
> *Joshua and the Flow of Biblical History*
>
> *Basic Bible Studies*
>
> *Art and the Bible*

———. *The Complete Works of Francis A. Schaeffer: A Christian Worldview*. Vol. 3, *A Christian View of Spirituality*. Westchester, Ill.: Crossway, 1982.

> *No Little People*
>
> *True Spirituality*
>
> *The New Super-Spirituality*
>
> *Two Contents, Two Realities*

———. *The Complete Works of Francis A. Schaeffer: A Christian Worldview*. Vol. 4, *A Christian View of the Church*. Westchester, Ill.: Crossway, 1982.

> *The Church at the End of the Twentieth Century*
>
> *The Church Before the Watching World*
>
> *The Mark of the Christian*
>
> *Death in the City*

———. *The Complete Works of Francis A. Schaeffer: A Christian Worldview*. Vol. 5, *A Christian View of the West*. Westchester, Ill.: Crossway, 1982.

Pollution and the Death of Man

How Should We Then Live?

Whatever Happened to the Human Race?

A Christian Manifesto

———. *The Great Evangelical Disaster.* Westchester, Ill.: Crossway, 1984.

Schuller, Robert H. *Prayer: My Soul's Adventure with God.* Nashville, Tenn.: Thomas Nelson Publishers, 1995.

Stoner, Peter W., and Robert C. Newman. *Science Speaks.* Chicago: Moody Press, 1976.

Trotter, W. F., M. L. Booth, and O. W. Wight, trans. *Harvard Classics: Thoughts and Minor Works of Pascal.* New York: Collier and Son, 1910.

Wessel, Helen. *The Autobiography of Charles Finney.* Minneapolis: Bethany House, 1977.

Wilson, Bill, comp. *The Best of Josh McDowell: A Ready Defense.* San Bernardino, Calif.: Here's Life Publishers, 1992.

Yancey, Philip. *Disappointment with God.* Grand Rapids, Mich.: Zondervan, 1988.

———. *Where Is God When It Hurts?* Grand Rapids, Mich.: Zondervan, 1978.

ABOUT THE AUTHOR

Becky Tirabassi is the author of the best-selling *Let Prayer Change Your Life*. Over the past ten years, Becky has written numerous inspirational and motivational books and has maintained an extensive national tour, speaking to every type and size of group—from 400 to 40,000. Becky's ongoing mission in life is to motivate and inspire people of all ages with her unique and exciting message that you can change your life! Becky and her husband live in Newport Beach, California.

If you would like more information on Becky's books, tapes, and seminars, please contact her at:

Change Your Life
P.O. Box 9672
Newport Beach, CA 92660
1-800-444-6189

A Winning Combination!

0-8407-9109-7 · Binder ·
276 pages

0-7852-7721-8 · Paperback ·
160 pages

0-7852-7746-3 · Paperback with
lay-flat binding · 256 pages

My Prayer Partner Notebook

Divided into sections for all aspects of prayer and worship, *My Partner Prayer Notebook* offers an easy-to-use system for building a disciplined prayer life. The binder format includes a daily schedule in half-hour increments, space for prayer requests and answers and reminders of "Things To Do." Refill pages also available.

Let Prayer Change Your Life and *Let Prayer Change Your Life Workbook*

A comprehensive and proven handbook on prayer that has already sold more than 100,000 copies. Tells how to use a prayer journal to strengthen commitment and to document the incredible results of focused prayer. Also available in a companion workbook.